D0875366

THE BORDERLAND
OF CRIMINAL
JUSTICE

THE BORDERLAND
OF CRIMINAL
JUSTICE

Essays in Law and Criminology

FRANCIS A. ALLEN

THE UNIVERSITY OF CHICAGO PRESS
Chicago and London

International Standard Book Number: 0–226–01416–9 (clothbound)
Library of Congress Catalog Card Number: 64–24972

THE UNIVERSITY OF CHICAGO PRESS, CHICAGO 60637
The University of Chicago Press, Ltd., London

To June

FOREWORD

A book consisting of essays that have already appeared in print requires an explanation; yet no explanation is likely to prove fully satisfying. In the course of the past decade I have committed to writing a series of lectures and occasional pieces which, in a quite unpremeditated way, develop a common theme or themes. Some of these essays attracted a measure of attention when first published. All discuss issues that seem to me important. I have persuaded myself that the collection displays a certain unity and that the individual items gain in significance when read as part of a whole. My justification is thus entirely conventional. Its merits must be left to the judgment and charity of the reader.

The rise of the sciences of human behavior is one of the most characteristic, perhaps one of the most important, products of modern thought. For many years it has been assumed by lawyers and non-lawyers alike that behavioral inquiry will produce, and ought to produce, a significant impact on the law and the operation of legal institutions. In consequence, a very substantial literature seeking to delineate the relations between behavioral science and the law has appeared. These essays make no effort to canvass the range of issues identified in the literature. Attention, instead, is focused on the area occupied by the criminal law and by legal institutions on the "borderland" of criminal justice. Although the essays touch on a variety of problems and issues, their uniting theme is perhaps adequately expressed by the proposition that appears near the conclusion of the first essay: "Our great problem today and for the future is to domesticate scientific knack and technique so that they may operate compatibly with the values and assumptions of a legal order and, at the same time, make their important contributions to our needs." These papers defend the proposition that the central problem of the criminal law is and will remain political in character. It is the problem of achieving the objectives of public order through the use of power so regulated as to preserve and nourish the basic political values.

The papers included in this volume appear in substantially their original form. Some minor changes of language have been made throughout in the interests of clarity. Because these essays appeared separately over a considerable period of time, bringing them together presented problems of repetition and overlap. I have attempted by revision to minimize these occurrences; but given the recurrence of the themes discussed in the various papers, the effort was not wholly successful. I am comforted by the thought that such overlap as survives may not be entirely undesirable. There are matters of argument and exposition that I might handle somewhat differently if I were to write these essays today, but I have made the decision to stand my ground and take my chances.

Since these essays present reflections extending over a decade, it is impossible to acknowledge fairly my indebtedness to the many persons who have provided help and stimulation. Any list would be partial and hence unjust. I can, however, acknowledge my gratitude to Mrs. Artie Scott, secretary par excellence, who prepared the typewritten manuscript. I also wish to express my appreciation to the various periodicals and institutions that generously consented to the reprinting of the essays in this volume.

CONTENTS

THE BORDERLAND
OF THE CRIMINAL LAW:

Problems of "Socializing" Criminal Justice

Modern psychology has made us all aware, perhaps too pain-
fully aware, of the numerous and intricate devices of self-
deception. And so, a student of the criminal law perhaps
indulges in self-deception when he asserts that there is
abroad today a new and important interest in the problems
of criminal justice and those of related fields. Only a few
years ago, the criminal-law professor was likely to conceive
of his role as that of a voice crying in the wilderness. The
situation, it must be conceded, has not altered basically in
the years since World War II. But at least today one vaguely
senses that the wilderness is more heavily populated than
heretofore.

The point need no longer be labored that the criminal
law and its administration are important—important
whether measured by the vital social interests the system is
intended to serve or by the impact of the system on the individual caught within its toils. It is high time, in these

Delivered as the second Sidney A. and Julia Teller Lecture, School
of Social Service Administration, University of Chicago, March 4,
1958. Printed in 32 SOCIAL SERVICE REV., 107–19 (1958). Reprinted
by permission.

areas, that we begin to appraise what we are doing and what we ought to be doing. Clearly, reappraisal and reconstruction cannot proceed far without the contributions of many professions and disciplines. Efforts to communicate across interdisciplinary barriers are being made. At best, however, these undertakings have proved tentative and sporadic; at worst, they have represented a kind of intellectual imperialism.

One of the objectives of the interdisciplinary conversation is a more rational definition of the roles that the various professional groups may be expected to perform. Lawyers and social workers, for example, may well be reminded that the distinction between penal treatment and the administration of welfare services is one that has sometimes been far from clear, even in theory. This is especially likely to be true in a culture that tends to conceive of poverty, unemployment, and even physical handicaps as evidence of a lack of moral fiber in those who suffer such misfortunes. A striking illustration of this tendency is the movement during the sixteenth and seventeenth centuries that led to the establishment, in England and on the Continent, of the so-called houses of correction. Two historians of this movement state: "The essence of the house of correction was that it combined the principles of the poorhouse, workhouse, and the penal institution."[1] Into these establishments were assembled, with spectacular abandon, the widows, the orphans, the jobless and handicapped, beggars, prostitutes, and petty criminals—all for the greater glory of God, the reduction of the poor rates, and the enhancement of statistics of national production. Who will say that in present practice we have fully divorced ourselves from similar motivations?

[1] RUSCHE & KIRCHHEIMER, PUNISHMENT AND SOCIAL STRUCTURE 42 (1939).

EFFECTS OF OVERBURDENING THE SYSTEM OF CRIMINAL JUSTICE

No one scrutinizing American criminal justice can fail to be impressed by the tremendous range of demands that are placed upon the system. This can be demonstrated in various ways. First, we may note the sheer bulk of penal regulations and observe the accelerating rate at which these accretions to the criminal law have occurred. Roscoe Pound once pointed out that "of one hundred thousand persons arrested in Chicago in 1912, more than one half were held for violation of legal precepts which did not exist twenty-five years before."[2] The tendency certainly has not slackened in the years since 1912. Thus, it has been estimated recently that "the number of crimes for which one may be prosecuted has at least doubled since the turn of the century."[3] More interesting than the mere volume of modern criminal legislation is the remarkable range of human activities now subject to the threat of criminal sanctions. Many years ago, before the most striking modern developments had occurred, the late Professor Ernst Freund remarked: "Living under free institutions we submit to public regulation and control in ways that appear inconceivable to the spirit of oriental despotism."[4] The killing of domesticated pigeons, the fencing of saltpeter caves against wandering cattle, the regulation of automobile traffic, the issue of daylight saving time versus

[2] CRIMINAL JUSTICE IN AMERICA 23 (1930).

[3] Laws, *Criminal Courts and Adult Probation*, 3 NPPA J. 354 (1957).

[4] STANDARDS OF AMERICAN LEGISLATION 21 (1917). Freund added: "It is well known what deep-seated repugnance and resistance of the native population to the invasion of their domestic privacy and personal habits English health officers in India have to overcome in order to enforce the sanitary measures necessary to prevent the spread of infection or contagious disease."

standard time, to give only a few examples, have all, at one place or another, been made problems of the criminal law. Moreover, we should not assume that this striking expansion of criminal liability has proceeded in a rational and orderly fashion or that, until recently, it has attracted any substantial amount of thoughtful and scholarly inquiry. The precise contrary is very nearly true. Thus, it is more than poetic metaphor to suggest that the system of criminal justice may be viewed as a weary Atlas upon whose shoulders we have heaped a crushing burden of responsibilities relating to public policy in its various aspects. This we have done thoughtlessly without inquiring whether the burden can be effectively borne.

The time has long been ripe for some sober questions to be asked. More and more it seems that the central issue may be this: What may we properly demand of a system of criminal justice? What functions may it properly serve? There is a related question: What are the obstacles and problems that must be confronted and overcome if a system of criminal justice is to be permitted to serve its own proper ends? These are broad and difficult questions, and the way in which they are answered will affect much that is important to the community at large.

As it has been suggested above, the system of criminal justice has sometimes been employed as a device for the administration of what are essentially social services. The consequences of this practice are almost always unfortunate. In this connection I shall advance a generalization, which I shall state somewhat dogmatically. Later I shall attempt to illustrate its application, even if I am unable to demonstrate fully its validity. The generalization is this: Whenever penal sanctions are employed to deal with problems of social service, two things are almost certain to happen and a third result may often occur. First, the social services will not be effectively rendered. Second, the diversion of personnel, resources, and energy required in the effort will adversely affect the ability of a system of criminal justice to fulfil those functions that it can perform. Finally, the effort may sometimes result in the corruption and demoralization of the agencies of criminal justice.

DETERIORATION OF SOCIAL SERVICES

My first assertion is that when the criminal law is relied upon to perform social services, those services are not likely to be effectively rendered. That there is a tendency to apply the criminal-law processes to such ends requires no elaborate demonstration. The crime of vagrancy, for example, represents, in one of its aspects, a primitive social reaction to the problems of human need. Perhaps, however, the point can best be conveyed by brief consideration of an actual situation. Some years ago I had occasion to visit a women's reformatory in an eastern state. Having been guided through the main structure of the institution—a rambling wooden building of Victorian vintage—I approached a rather modern brick establishment, located some distance away. As I entered the door, I suddenly discovered that I was standing in a nursery. On both sides of the room were rows of cribs, each crib occupied by an infant of an age ranging from three to eighteen months. These were children of women prisoners, born while their mothers were in penal custody. In almost every case the mothers were unwed and had been sentenced to the reformatory following conviction for some offense relating to extra-marital sexual relations. As I began to react to this spectacle, I was led to the obvious inquiry: Why are there so *few* infants here? Surely, these babies represent only the smallest fraction of the total number of illegitimate children born each year in this populous state. The answer to this question is significant and characteristic. These were unwed mothers without the financial resources to pay for the medical expenses of childbirth or the subsequent care of their offspring. True enough, the state had made funds available to local public agencies for the care of such mothers and their children. But these funds were not fully compensatory. Accordingly, some localities soon discovered that it was cheaper, when measured by immediate budgetary considerations, to proceed criminally against such women, thereby shifting the full burden of their provision and care from the locality to the state.

I tell this story not because it is unusual. It is, on the contrary, illustrative of much that we do. The presence of these women and their children in a penal institution cannot be explained by any viable state policy directed to the punishment of extra-marital relations. They are there because they are paupers or because the local officials were unable to force payment of the expenses of childbirth and care on the responsible male party. Criminal processes are rarely considered when the unwed mother has financial resources of her own or is able to secure aid from her family or friends. Unlike other ages, we do not react to the problem of the unwed mother by stoning the woman and subjecting the infant to death by exposure. But we do on occasion administer our social services through the agencies of the criminal law. One may wonder about the quality of services that result in stamping the stigma of a felony conviction on the mother and providing the child in its first impressionable months with the environment of a prison nursery. But this is not all.

There is a further consideration that I can characterize only as an issue of justice. When penal treatment is employed to perform the functions of social service, selection of those eligible for penal treatment proceeds on inadmissible criteria. Persons are selected for criminal conviction not by reference to their moral character or social dangerousness but by reference to their poverty or their helplessness. Thus, we may object that such use of the penal process does not result in effective performance of the social-service function. We may also object that it lacks equity and decency.

IMPAIRMENT OF LAW ENFORCEMENT

My second proposition is this: Whenever the system of criminal justice is burdened with functions it cannot effectively perform, one consequence is the diversion of energies and resources from those vital functions of public order that the criminal law, and only the criminal law, can perform. Here, surely, is the source of much of the frustration that characterizes American law enforcement. Consider for a moment the burdens cast upon the system by such a problem as that of habitual drunkenness and alcoholic addiction. In 1956, the Chicago police are reported to have made 77,825 arrests for drunkenness, the largest number for any offense except automobile traffic violations.[5] That this figure is not abnormally large is indicated by the fact that, in the same year, the Los Angeles police department made 98,707 arrests for drunkenness and that in the three years from 1954 through 1956 arrests for drunkenness in Los Angeles constituted between 43 and 46 per cent of all arrest bookings.[6]

[5] 1957 CHICAGO POLICE ANN. REP. 15.

[6] 1954 LOS ANGELES POLICE ANN. REP. 31; 1955 ANN. REP. 31; 1956 ANN. REP. 31.

Actually, these figures greatly understate the magnitude of the police problem. They do not measure the expenditure of police effort that does not result in formal arrests for drunkenness. They do not adequately convey the burden cast upon the courts or on the jail and detention facilities. They do not even fully describe the arrest situation, since habitual drunkenness and alcoholism may be important factors in arrests for such crimes as vagrancy, disorderly conduct, and the like.[7]

If all of this effort, all of this investment of time and money, were producing constructive results, then we might find satisfaction in the situation despite its costs. But the fact is that this activity accomplishes little that is fundamental. No one can seriously suggest that the threat of fines and jail sentences actually deters habitual drunkenness or alcoholic addiction. There are instances of the same person being arrested as many as forty times in a single year on charges of drunkenness, and every large urban center can point to cases of individuals appearing before the courts on such charges 125, 150, or even 200 times in the course of a somewhat longer period. Nor, despite the heroic efforts being made in a few localities,[8] is there much reason to suppose that any very effective measures of cure and therapy can or will be administered in the jails. But the weary proc-

[7] In 208 cities of over 25,000 population, 677,808 arrests for drunkenness, disorderly conduct, and vagrancy were reported in 1952. There were 497,218 convictions for these offenses (24 FED. BUREAU OF INVESTIGATION, UNIFORM CRIME REP. 59 [1953]).

[8] Efforts at rehabilitation of alcoholics within the jail system have been made, for example, in Los Angeles. The program of the San Rita Rehabilitation Center, Alameda County, California, is briefly described in an address by Myrl E. Alexander, *Trends in Jail Administration in Metropolitan Communities*, in PAPERS FROM CITIZENS CONFERENCE ON THE COOK COUNTY JAIL AND CORRECTIONAL TREATMENT (1956).

ess continues, to the detriment of the total performance of the law-enforcement function.

CORRUPTION OF AGENCIES OF CRIMINAL JUSTICE

The third proposition in the generalization advanced above is that the consequences of forcing certain incompatible obligations on the system of penal justice may sometimes contribute to the corruption of the agencies of criminal justice. Every American criminal code identifies as eligible for penal treatment persons who indulge in certain types of conduct that might better be left to the exclusive concern of medicine, psychiatry, or the general moral sense of the community. Consider, for example, the matter of voluntary homosexual relations between adult participants.[9] Such behavior is generally made punishable in American law, sometimes by sanctions of extreme severity.[10] If the objective of such laws is to prevent homosexual behavior, they have surely failed in their purpose.[11] But these laws have other consequences, few of them desirable. One need not be overly so-

[9] For a recent survey of these problems at the official level, see COMMITTEE ON HOMOSEXUAL OFFENSES AND PROSTITUTION REP. CMD. No. 247 (1957). See also Glueck, *An Evaluation of the Homosexual Offender*, 41 MINN. L. REV. 187–210 (1957).

[10] ILLINOIS COMMISSION ON SEX OFFENDERS REP. 28 (1953). "Homosexual practices are specifically condemned in virtually all the state codes. Sodomy has been made a felony in all but two states. Punishments range from a possible minimum fine of $100 in Indiana to a possible maximum sentence of thirty years imprisonment in five other states." See also Bensing, *A Comparative Study of American Sex Statutes*, 42 J. CRIM. L., C. & P.S. 63–64 (1951).

[11] The incidence of homosexual contacts is exhaustively surveyed in KINSEY, POMEREY & MARTIN, SEXUAL BEHAVIOR IN THE HUMAN MALE 610 (1948). See also Committee report, cited *supra* note 9, at 17–20.

phisticated to understand that perhaps the most tangible result of this legislation is to place in the hands of unscrupulous police officers and others an instrument of blackmail by which money and property can be extorted from the homosexual under threat of exposure and prosecution. This ugly and unpleasant situation has been reported in urban communities throughout the country.[12] Indeed, the proposition may be broadened. Almost every case in which the law calls upon the enforcement agencies to stamp out conduct that involves a willing seller and a willing buyer—or, more fundamentally, conduct in which the "victim," if there is one, is a willing victim—is a situation that contains the seeds of police corruption and demoralization. These instances include such crimes as voluntary sexual relations between adults, gambling, and sales of liquor and narcotics. In all such categories the police are confronted with extraordinary difficulties in obtaining evidence of violations. All too often the difficulties of enforcement provide the police with strong temptations to obtain evidence by the use of illegitimate means. So it is here that we are most likely to encounter the unscrupulous undercover agent,[13] the illegal arrest,[14] the unreasonable search and seizure,[15] the unlawful use of electronic equipment.[16] It is not my point that all laws making

[12] A discussion of the experience in New York is presented in PLOSCOWE, SEX AND THE LAW 209–10 (1951). See also AMERICAN LAW INSTITUTE, MODEL PENAL CODE 279 (Tent. Draft No. 4, 1955). *Cf.* Kelly v. United States, 194 F. 2d 150 (D.C. Cir. 1952).

[13] Sorrels v. United States, 287 U.S. 435 (1932) (illegal sale of liquor).

[14] Johnson v. United States, 333 U.S. 10 (1948) (narcotics offense).

[15] Irvine v. California, 347 U.S. 128 (1954) (gambling offense).

[16] Olmstead v. United States, 277 U.S. 438 (1928) (violation of the National Prohibition Act).

such acts criminal can or should be repealed; but it seems wholly responsible to assert that we have entered into such areas of penal regulation with too little reflection and with too little calculation of the costs.

DIFFICULTIES IN MODIFYING THE SYSTEM

This, then, is my generalization: The determination of what sorts of functions are to be delegated to the institutions of criminal justice is of prime importance to the agencies of the criminal law. Moreover, such determination profoundly affects the broad areas of human welfare located at the borderland of the criminal law. I claim no particular novelty for these propositions. Indeed, these considerations, although rarely articulated, are very close to the heart of the widespread dissatisfaction with American criminal justice that has been expressed for a half-century and longer. Moreover, this dissatisfaction has resulted in concrete measures. Functions have been stripped from the system of criminal justice and located in other official agencies or, sometimes, in private hands. We have, for example, attempted to eliminate the predominantly punitive orientation in the handling of juvenile misbehavior by establishing a new kind of court for the trial of juvenile cases. We have devised other procedures to deal with what are conceived to be essentially medical and psychiatric problems. For all this activity, however, reform of criminal justice has been slow and painful. Furthermore, in devising new techniques and procedures we have encountered new problems almost as intractable as the old dilemmas. Thus, there are two further questions which we should ask: First, why has fundamental reform of the system of criminal justice been delayed so long? Second, what peculiar dangers and perils lurk in the path of such reform?

INADEQUATE KNOWLEDGE AND TECHNIQUES

When we ask why we have been so slow in stripping incompatible functions from the agencies of criminal justice and why we have been so ineffectual in devising "better ways" of doing things, eager diagnosticians are likely to step forward with familiar and pat answers. We shall be told that progress is obstructed by the lack of public interest and support and by the absence of adequate funds. That these factors are real and their consequences devastating few would care to deny. Yet, these familiar scapegoats do not provide the most fundamental explanations. We should not overlook the fact that, in many areas, our basic difficulties still lie in our ignorance of human behavior in its infinite complexities. I have referred to the burdens placed on the police function by the problem of drunkenness and alcoholic addiction. In large measure we handle these problems so badly because we do not know how to handle them better.[17] To be sure, there is much room for improvement in such matters as the facilities and surroundings in which persons detained for drunkenness are confined. No doubt, on a selective basis,

[17] In this connection, the development of public-financed clinics for the treatment or rehabilitation of the alcoholic should be noted. An outstanding example is the pioneering experiment made in the District of Columbia, Public Law 347 (80th Cong., 1st Sess.), 61 Stat. 744 (1947), D.C. Code §§24–501–514. An interesting appraisal of experience under the law may be found in Wexberg, *The Outpatient Treatment of Alcoholism in the District of Columbia*, 14 Q. J. of Studies on Alcohol 514–24 (1953). The author says, *inter alia:* "The relief for police, courts and penal authorities has not materialized. . . . The destitute alcoholic, who is at the same time the chronic repeater at the court, can be reached only to a small degree by an outpatient facility." For a report on the Connecticut clinics, see Brunner-Orne, Iddings & Rodrigues, *A Court Clinic for Alcoholics*, 12 Q. J. of Studies on Alcohol 592–600 (1951).

individuals could be salvaged who are presently not receiving the sympathetic and intelligent attention that might prove sufficient to the attainment of that happy result.[18] But a fundamental solution to the problems posed by alcoholism awaits further understanding of the affliction and the devising of reasonably reliable, inexpensive, and expeditious therapy. Unless I misread the literature of the field, we are still far from these desirable goals, despite the substantial quantity of impressive and creative research now being carried forward. What is true of alcoholism is also true of such areas as narcotic addiction, although it must be conceded that it requires more than a reference to scientific ignorance to justify the absurdities of current efforts to control the narcotics traffic in the United States.[19]

Ignorance, of itself, is disgraceful only so far as it is avoidable. But when, in our eagerness to find "better ways" of handling old problems, we rush to measures affecting human liberty and human personality on the assumption that we have knowledge which, in fact, we do not possess, then the problem of ignorance takes on a more sinister hue. One of the most alarming aspects of the current agitation for reform of criminal justice and related areas is the apparent willingness of some proponents of reform to substitute action for knowledge—action of the sort that often results in the most serious consequences to the affected individuals. Unfortunately, this is a tendency found only too frequently among lawyers of the more "progressive" variety. Let me be

[18] REA, ALCOHOLISM: ITS PSYCHOLOGY AND CURE (1956).

[19] It seems fair to say that American official efforts to deal with the problems of narcotics traffic and addiction are more and more committed to a policy of repression involving sanctions of ever greater severity. For general reference consult *Narcotics: A Symposium*, 22 LAW & CONTEMP. PROB. 1–154 (1957).

concrete. Since 1938, legislatures of nearly one-third of the states have adopted so-called sexual psychopath laws.[20] These statutes provide for the commitment and indeterminate confinement of persons, usually, but not always, described as "sexual psychopaths." The definition of that crucial term varies somewhat from state to state, but it is intended to describe persons likely, in the future, to commit dangerous sex acts. Many of the statutes reflect that interesting exercise in word-magic which results in labeling procedures "civil" rather than "criminal."[21] These laws characteristically require that a person so committed shall receive "treatment" while incarcerated.[22] Some direct that the person shall be released only when he is "cured."[23] All of these provisions rest on certain assumptions of fact. First, they

[20] The first of these statutes appears to have been enacted in Michigan in 1937. However, it was declared unconstitutional in substantial part the following year. People v. Frontczak, 286 Mich. 51, 281 N.W. 534 (1938). The earliest statute to survive constitutional attack became law in Illinois in 1938 (ILL. REV. STAT., ch. 38, §§820–25 [1939]). A chart comparing the provisions of many of the state statutes will be found in ILLINOIS COMMISSION ON SEX OFFENDERS REP. 33–35.

[21] See, *e.g.*, MINN. STAT. ANN., §§526.09–10 (1947); ILL. REV. STAT., ch. 38, §822.01 (1957).

[22] "The Director of Public Safety as guardian shall provide care and treatment for the person committed to him designed to effect recovery." (ILL. REV. STAT., ch. 38, §825a [1957]).

[23] See, *e.g.*, CAL. WELFARE AND INSTITUTIONS CODE, §5519 (Deering 1952): "If the court finds that the person has recovered from his sexual psychopathy to such an extent that he is no longer a menace to the health and safety of others, or that he will not benefit by further care and treatment in the hospital and is not a menace to the health and safety of others, the committing court shall thereafter cause the person to be returned to the court in which the criminal charge was tried to await further action with reference to such criminal charge."

assume a body of knowledge and technique that enables its practitioners to identify with reasonable accuracy those persons likely to commit dangerous sexual acts in the future and to exclude with reasonable certainty those posing no such danger. If this assumption is false, if there is no such knowledge or technique, these laws, when applied, present the grave threat of depriving persons who constitute no serious threat to the community of their liberty. Second, these laws assume that there is a therapy adequate to treat and cure the sexual psychopath, once he has been committed to an institution. If this assumption is false, these statutes are not rehabilitative measures, whatever verbalisms may be employed to describe them. Third, these statutes assume, not only that such knowledge and technique exist, but that, as a practical matter, they are available to the state in the administration of these laws. I shall content myself by saying that many competent observers doubt that any of these assumptions are able to bear the weight of fair and impartial investigation.[24]

At least one great man of antiquity taught that the beginning of wisdom is the consciousness of ignorance. If this be true, there is no paradox in the assertion that the real utility of scientific technique in the fields under discussion is dependent on an accurate realization of the limits of scientific knowledge. Arrogance here is far too expensive a luxury to be tolerated, for the most important of individual

[24] For critical discussions of the sexual psychopath legislation, consult Sutherland, *The Sexual Psychopath Laws*, 40 J. Crim. L., C. & P.S. 543–54 (1950); Hacker & Frym, *The Sexual Psychopath Act in Practice: A Critical Discussion*, 43 Cal. L. Rev. 766–80 (1955); Guttmacher & Weihofen, *Sex Offenses*, 43 J. Crim. L., C. & P.S. 153–75 (1952); Orenstein, *The Sex Offender*, in National Probation and Parole Association Year Book, 195–220 (1950).

values are at stake: human liberty and human dignity. Those of us who are members of professions concerned with influencing and regulating human behavior need to remind ourselves of these things. Of us, in particular, it is required that our actions be tempered by a wise and decent humility.

THREATS TO PROCEDURAL SAFEGUARDS

For one interested in identifying the dilemmas and perils associated with a fundamental redefinition of the system of criminal justice, no development is of greater significance than the juvenile court movement. This is true both because the problems associated with juvenile misconduct are themselves of pressing urgency and because our efforts to deal with them at the official level, outside the traditional agencies of criminal justice, have identified issues of practice and principle of even broader concern. The establishment of the first juvenile court over half a century ago was prompted by an explicit dissatisfaction with the agencies of the criminal law.[25] The measures taken in response were intended to be radical and fundamental. The entire concept of crime was deemed inapplicable to juvenile misconduct; instead, a new label, delinquency, was devised. Provision was made for a new kind of tribunal, non-punitive in orientation, and one designed to help rather than to punish. To secure these ends, the resources of psychiatry, social work, and sociological technique were to be employed.[26] These were

[25] The first state statute establishing a juvenile court was adopted in Illinois. "An Act To Regulate the Treatment and Conduct of Dependent, Neglected and Delinquent Children," approved April 21, 1899 (Ill. Sess. Laws 1899 121).

[26] See the sponsoring REP. COMMITTEE OF THE CHICAGO B. A. (1899): "The fundamental idea of the law is that the state must

lofty goals, and one's sympathy with such objectives is in no way inconsistent with a candid recognition that, in practice, they have been rarely fully attained. My purpose, however, is not to appraise the success of the juvenile court movement. It is, rather, to inquire what matters of general significance can be derived from this long and often conscientious effort.

The essential spirit of the juvenile court has never been better expressed than in a statement made by the late Judge Edward F. Waite more than four decades ago. According to Judge Waite, the crucial distinction between the traditional criminal court and the juvenile court is that between a court which directs its efforts "to do something *to* a child because of what he *has done*," and a court concerned with "doing something for a child because of what he *is* and *needs*."[27] This distinction, so felicitously expressed, points to very real

---

step in and exercise guardianship over a child found under such adverse social or individual conditions as develop crime. . . . It proposes a plan whereby he may be treated, not as a criminal, or legally charged with crime, but as a ward of the state, to receive practically the care, custody and discipline that are accorded the neglected and dependent child, and which as the act states, 'shall approximate as nearly as may be that which should be given by its parents.' " See also Killian, *The Juvenile Court as an Institution*, 261 ANNALS 89–100 (1949) ; and Schramm, *Philosophy of the Juvenile Court*, 261 ANNALS 101–8 (1949).

[27] The statement in full is as follows: "The Court which must direct its procedure even apparently to do something *to* a child because of what he *has done*, is parted from the court which is avowedly concerned only with doing something *for* a child because of what he *is* and *needs*, by a gulf too wide to be bridged by any humanity which the judge may introduce into his hearings, or by the habitual use of corrective rather than punitive methods after conviction." Waite, *How Far Can Court Procedures Be Socialized without Impairing Individual Rights?* 12 J. CRIM. L., C. & P.S. 340 (1921).

and significant differences in orientation. The difficulty is that too often the distinctions between doing something *to* and *for* a child are misconceived and the resulting confusion produces attitudes and procedures inimical, not only to the attainment of the proper objectives of the juvenile court movement, but to the preservation and strengthening of broader human values.

It is important, first, to recognize that when, in an authoritative setting, we attempt to do something *for* a child "because of what he is and needs," we are also doing something *to* him. The semantics of "socialized justice" are a trap for the unwary. Whatever one's motivations, however elevated one's objectives, if the measures taken result in the compulsory loss of the child's liberty, the involuntary separation of a child from his family, or even the supervision of a child's activities by a probation worker, the impact on the affected individuals is essentially a punitive one. Good intentions and a flexible vocabulary do not alter this reality. This is particularly so when, as is often the case, the institution to which the child is committed is, in fact, a peno-custodial establishment. We shall escape much confusion here if we are willing to give candid recognition to the fact that the business of the juvenile court inevitably consists, to a considerable degree, in dispensing punishment. If this is true, we can no more avoid the problem of unjust punishment in the juvenile court than in the criminal court.

There is a second sort of confusion that stems from the distinction between doing something to and for a child. All too often it is forgotten that, for the purpose of determining what a child *is*, it may be highly important to know what he has actually done. For this reason, if for no other, we cannot afford to be careless in establishing the facts of his conduct. This point has broader application than to the procedures of the juvenile court. This interesting case is said to have occurred in California: A defendant was convicted of a sexual offense. He was subsequently committed as a sexual psychopath after a psychiatric examination. In making their diagnosis the psychiatrists *assumed* that the defendant had committed the sexual act which provided the basis for the criminal conviction. The difficulty was that, as later established, the defendant had all along been the victim of misidentification. Thus, the mistake as to the facts not only resulted in an improper conviction but rendered invalid the psychiatric judgment of the defendant's personality and propensities.[28] However advanced our techniques for determining what an individual *is*, we have not yet approached the point at which we can safely ignore what he has done. What he has done may often be the most revealing evidence of what he is.

Finally, we cannot escape the question of what the child has done, because we cannot prudently ignore the sense of injustice that will surely be engendered in the child by carelessness in establishing the facts of his behavior. A child brought before a tribunal, more or less specifically charged with commission of particular acts, will feel, and I believe will properly feel, that he has the right to receive from the court a sober and cautious weighing of the evidence relating to that issue. He has, in short, a right to receive not only the benevolent concern of the tribunal but justice. One may question with reason the value of therapy purchased at the expense of justice.

As the years have passed, it has become increasingly apparent that there are certain problems and principles of de-

[28] Hacker & Frym, *op. cit. supra* note 24.

cent procedure that survive changes in the form of tribunals and the shifting orientation of our efforts. To be sure, courts have occasionally expressed the view that children, being "wards of the state," have no legal rights that the juvenile court is bound to respect.[29] Such an attitude, while still revealed frequently enough in practice, is given formal expression less often today than in years gone by. There is, I believe, a wider understanding that the due-process concept represents something more than outmoded ritual or a lawyer's quibble. This is true, perhaps, because we all—lawyers and non-lawyers alike—have seen enough of the twentieth-century world to render untenable any assumption of the inevitable benevolence of state power. Moreover, at a more practical level, we have had occasion to discover that the exercise of arbitrary and undisciplined power in the juvenile courts has retarded rather than advanced attainment of the objectives of the juvenile court movement.

What the obligations of decent procedure are in the context of the juvenile court is still a matter of acrimonious debate. There are, it seems to me, certain indispensable conditions. First, we need greater clarity in the definition of the jurisdiction of the juvenile courts. Surely, when great powers over the lives and liberties of persons are granted—even when the persons are merely children—it should be possible

---

[29] Thus, in a case in which a fifteen-year-old girl was committed to a reform school merely on the application of her parents, the court said: "The child, herself, having no right to control her own action or to select her own course of life, had no legal right to be heard in these proceedings. Hence, the law which does not require her to be brought in person before the committing officer or extend her the privilege of a hearing on her own behalf cannot be said to deprive her of the benefit of due process of law" (Rule v. Geddes, 23 App. D.C. 31, 50 [1904]). See Paulsen, *Fairness to the Juvenile Offender*, 41 MINN. L. REV. 547–76 (1957).

to determine with reasonable certainty what the limits of
these powers are. This is as important to the conscientious
judge who wields the power as it is to the child or his parents who may be affected by it. Yet it is true that in many
jurisdictions the statutory definitions of even the basic terms
"delinquent" or "delinquency" are so amorphous and so
all-inclusive that little practical guidance is actually provided.[30] It may be conceded that the definition of "delinquency" can hardly be stated with the precision of a legal
description in a real estate deed, but this does not mean that
a meaningful and reasonable definition of the powers of the
tribunal cannot be achieved.

Second, we must by all means be concerned with the
quality and quantity of evidence required to establish the
delinquent status of the child. One need not insist that the
hearsay rule in all its rigor be bodily transported into juvenile court proceedings.[31] The essential point is that, before

[30] The Illinois definition of the term "delinquent child," before
legislative alterations in 1963, illustrates the proposition (ILL. REV.
STAT., ch. 23, §2001 [1957]). See also TAPPAN, JUVENILE DE-
LINQUENCY 202–3 (1949).

[31] *Cf.* Waite, *op. cit. supra* note 27, at 343: "Rules of ancient
origin, approved or at least tolerated by the citizen whenever he
resorts to other legal forums to assert or defend his rights, should
not lightly be set aside in juvenile courts. The only safe practice is
to observe them. If hearsay, for example, has not been found justly
admissible in civil disputes and criminal trials, it is no better in
juvenile court proceedings. Exceptions should be made when appropriate, and informal short cuts will often be found agreeable to
all concerned; but the exception should always be regarded as an
exception. No judge on any bench has need to be more thoroughly
grounded in the principles of evidence and more constantly mindful
of them than the judge of a juvenile court." For a striking instance
of resort to hearsay evidence in a juvenile court proceeding, see
Holmes's Appeal, 379 Pa. 599, 109 A 2d 523 (1954).

the child can properly be subjected to the drastic powers of the court, more than gossip and rumor is required to establish his legal eligibility for such treatment.[32] This further implies that restrictions must be imposed on the use of social casework reports when the issue is whether the child committed the acts charged against him. If such reports are to be employed at all for this purpose, counsel for the child should be given the names of those supplying information to the investigator and should have the right to call such persons into court for cross-examination. This is, of course, a vexed issue, and the position that I have taken involves certain costs by way of loss of confidentiality. If the centuries of experience in the trial of cases before the common-law courts have any lesson to teach, it is that human testimony is often tainted with errors of perception, memory, bias, and prejudice. The most important protections against such errors yet devised, and they are by no means infallible, are confrontation and cross-examination. Out-of-court statements made in private to a caseworker, however useful for other purposes, do not afford an appropriate basis for determining whether the charges made against a child are true or false. They must also be treated with appropriate caution when considered in connection with the issue of disposition after the delinquency of the child has been established.

Finally, I believe that the minimum requirements of decent procedure in the juvenile court include recognition of a right to counsel on behalf of the child and perhaps of the

[32] There is considerable literature on the point. Among the most helpful are Paulsen, *op. cit.*; Diana, *The Rights of Juvenile Delinquents: An Appraisal of Juvenile Court Procedures*, 47 J. CRIM. L., C. & P.S. 561–69 (1957). See also Tappan, *Unofficial Delinquency*, 29 NEB. L. REV. 547 (1950). See also JUSTICE FOR THE CHILD (Ronsenheim ed. 1962).

child's parents. This is not to deny that many lawyers operate ineffectually in this environment, nor is it possible to deny that lawyers tend to make nuisances of themselves wherever they may be. But there is no reason whatever to doubt that in many cases the attainment of a fair hearing in the juvenile court requires legal representation of the child as insistently as in any other tribunal. There are two further reasons for greater participation by attorneys in juvenile court proceedings. In the first place, it is good for an institution to have on the premises persons sufficiently independent and sufficiently brash to challenge, on occasion, the assumptions and methods of the institution. I know of no better therapy for the messianic complex. Second, greater familiarity of the bar as a whole with the juvenile court and its problems would probably provide the institution with the support of an important segment of public opinion now too frequently denied it.

It is my contention that the improvement of criminal justice involves, among other things, the stripping from the system of some of the functions it is now called upon to perform. Many of these tasks, if not assumed by the system of criminal justice, will have to be undertaken by other official agencies. If these changes are to be salutary, it must be recognized that there are standards of decency and dignity that apply whenever human liberty and volition are affected. These obligations are in no way obliterated or minimized by a change in the tribunal, the name of the procedure, or the methods employed. Our great problem today and for the future is to domesticate scientific knack and technique so that they may operate compatibly with the values and assumptions of a legal order and, at the same time, make their important contributions to our needs. Stating the problem, of course, does not resolve it, but a general recognition that this is our problem would represent a substantial gain. Above all, we cannot afford to be lured into the belief that good intentions are a sufficient substitute for procedural fairness. Indeed, it may almost be true that the naïve man of good intentions is more dangerous in this area than the knave, for the latter at least may be constrained by the consciousness of guilt. Reform, improvement, and progress we all devoutly seek. But a healthy caveat was uttered twenty-five hundred years ago. The Greek philosopher, Heraclitus is reported to have said: "False opinions of progress are the enemies of progress."

LEGAL VALUES AND THE
REHABILITATIVE IDEAL

Although one is sometimes inclined to despair of any constructive changes in the administration of criminal justice, a glance at the history of the past half-century reveals a succession of the most significant developments. Thus, the last fifty years have seen the widespread acceptance of three legal inventions of great importance: the juvenile court, systems of probation, and systems of parole. During the same period, under the inspiration of Continental research and writing, scientific criminology has become an established field of instruction and inquiry in American universities and in other research agencies. At the same time, psychiatry has made its remarkable contributions to the theory of human behavior and, more specifically, to that form of human behavior described as criminal. These developments have been accompanied by nothing less than a revolution in public conceptions of the nature of crime and the criminal and in public attitudes toward the proper treatment of the convicted offender.

This history with its complex developments of thought,

First delivered as a lecture at the Institute for Juvenile Research, Chicago, Illinois, on March 17, 1959, and printed in 50 J. Crim. L., C. & P.S. 226–32 (1959). Reprinted by permission.

institutional behavior, and public attitudes must be approached gingerly; for in dealing with it we are in peril of committing the sin of oversimplification. Nevertheless, despite the presence of contradictions and paradox, it seems possible to detect one common element in much of this thought and activity which goes far to characterize the history we are considering. This common element or theme I shall describe, for want of a better phrase, as the rise of the rehabilitative ideal.

The rehabilitative ideal is itself a complex of ideas which, perhaps, defies an exact definition. The essential points, however, can be identified. It is assumed, first, that human behavior is the product of antecedent causes. These causes can be identified as part of the physical universe, and it is the obligation of the scientist to discover and to describe them with all possible exactitude. Knowledge of the antecedents of human behavior makes possible an approach to the scientific control of human behavior. Finally, and of primary significance for the purposes at hand, it is assumed that measures employed to treat the convicted offender should serve a therapeutic function; that such measures should be designed to effect changes in the behavior of the convicted person in the interests of his own happiness, health, and satisfactions and in the interest of social defense.

Although these ideas are capable of quite simple statement, they have provoked some of the modern world's most acrimonious controversies. And the disagreements among those who adhere in general to these propositions have been hardly less intense than those prompted by the dissenters. This is true, in part, because these ideas possess a delusive simplicity. No idea is more pervaded with ambiguity than the notion of reform or rehabilitation. Assuming, for example, that we have the techniques to accomplish our ends of rehabilitation, are we striving to produce in the convicted offender something called "adjustment" to his social environment or is our objective something different from or more than this? By what scale of values do we determine the ends of therapy?[1]

These are intriguing questions, well worth extended consideration. But it is not my purpose to pursue them here. Rather, I am concerned with describing some of the dilemmas and conflicts of values that have resulted from efforts to impose the rehabilitative ideal on the system of criminal justice. There is no area in which a more effective demonstration can be made of the necessity for greater mutual understanding between the law and the behavioral disciplines.

There is, of course, nothing new in the notion of reform or rehabilitation of the offender as being one objective of the penal process. This idea is given important emphasis, for example, in the thought of the medieval churchmen. The church's position, as described by Sir Francis Palgrave, was that punishment was not to be "thundered in vengeance for the satisfaction of the state, but imposed for the good of the offender: in order to afford the means of amendment and to lead the transgressor to repentance, and to mercy."[2] Even Jeremy Bentham, whose views modern criminologists have often scorned and more often ignored, is found saying: "It is a great merit in a punishment to contribute to the *refor-*

[1] "We see that it is not easy to determine what we consider to be the sickness and what we consider to be the cure." FROMM, PSYCHO-ANALYSIS AND RELIGION 73 (1950). See also the author's development of these points at 67–77.

[2] Quoted in DALZELL, BENEFIT OF CLERGY AND RELATED MATTERS 13 (1955).

mation of the offender, not only through fear of being punished again, but by a change in his character and habits."[3] But this is far from saying that the modern expression of the rehabilitative ideal is not to be sharply distinguished from earlier expressions. The most important differences, I believe, are two. First, the modern statement of the rehabilitative ideal is accompanied by, and largely stems from, the development of scientific disciplines concerned with human behavior, a development not remotely approximated in earlier periods when notions of reform of the offender were advanced. Second, and of equal importance for the purposes at hand, in no other period has the rehabilitative ideal so completely dominated theoretical and scholarly inquiry, to such an extent that in some quarters it is almost assumed that matters of treatment and reform of the offender are the only questions worthy of serious attention in the whole field of criminal justice and corrections.

The Narrowing of Scientific Interests

This narrowing of interests prompted by the rise of the rehabilitative ideal during the past half-century should put us on our guard. No social institutions as complex as those involved in the administration of criminal justice serve a sin-

[3] BENTHAM, THE THEORY OF LEGISLATION 338–39 (Ogden ed. 1931). (Italics in the original.) But Bentham added: "But when [the writers] come to speak about the means of preventing offenses, of rendering men better, of perfecting morals, their imagination grows warm, their hopes excited; one would suppose they were about to produce the great secret, and that the human race was going to receive a new form. It is because we have a more magnificent idea of objects in proportion as they are less familiar, and because the imagination has a loftier flight amid vague projects which have never been subjected to the limits of analysis." *Id.* at 359.

gle function or purpose. Social institutions are multivalued and multipurposed. Values and purposes are likely on occasion to prove inconsistent and to produce internal conflict and tension. A theoretical orientation that evinces concern for only one or a limited number of the purposes served by the institution must inevitably prove partial and unsatisfactory. In certain situations it may prove positively dangerous. This stress on the unfortunate consequences of the rise of the rehabilitative ideal need not involve failure to recognize the substantial benefits that have also accompanied its emergence. Its emphasis on the fundamental problems of human behavior, its numerous contributions to the decency of the criminal-law processes are of vital importance. But the limitations and dangers of modern trends of thought need to be clearly identified in the interest, among others, of the rehabilitative ideal itself.

My first proposition is that the rise of the rehabilitative ideal has dictated what questions are to be investigated, with the result that many matters of equal or even greater importance have been ignored or insufficiently examined. This tendency can be abundantly illustrated. Thus, the concentration of interest on the nature and needs of the criminal has resulted in a remarkable absence of interest in the nature of crime. This is, indeed, surprising, for on reflection it must be apparent that the question of what is a crime is logically the prior issue: how crime is defined determines in large measure who the criminal is who becomes eligible for treatment and therapy.[4] A related observation was made some years ago by the late Karl Llewellyn: "When I was younger I used to hear smuggish assertions among my socio-

---

[4] *Cf.* Hart, *The Aims of the Criminal Law,* 23 LAW & CONTEMP. PROB. 401 (1958).

logical friends, such as: 'I take the sociological, *not* the legal, approach to crime'; and I suspect an inquiring reporter could still hear much the same (perhaps with 'psychiatric' often substituted for 'sociological')—though it is surely somewhat obvious that when you take 'the legal' out, you also take out 'crime.' "[5] This disinterest in the definition of criminal behavior has afflicted the lawyers quite as much as the behavioral scientists. Even the criminal law scholar has tended, until recently, to assume that problems of procedure and treatment are the things that "really matter." Only the issue of criminal responsibility as affected by mental disorder has attracted the consistent attention of the nonlawyer, and the literature reflecting this interest is not remarkable for its cogency or its wisdom. In general, the behavioral sciences have left other issues relevant to crime definition largely in default. There are a few exceptions. Dr. Hermann Mannheim, of the London School of Economics, has manifested intelligent interest in these matters.[6] The late Professor Edwin Sutherland's studies of "white-collar crime" may also be mentioned, although, in my judgment, Professor Sutherland's efforts in this field are among the least perceptive and satisfactory of his many valuable contributions.[7]

The absence of widespread interest in these areas is not to be explained by any lack of challenging questions. Thus, what may be said of the relationships between legislative

[5] *Law and the Social Sciences—Especially Sociology*, 62 HARV. L. REV. 1286, 1287 (1949).

[6] See, especially, his CRIMINAL JUSTICE AND SOCIAL RECONSTRUCTION (1946).

[7] WHITE-COLLAR CRIME (1949). See also CLINARD, THE BLACK MARKET (1952). *Cf.* Caldwell, *A Re-examination of the Concept of White-Collar Crime*, 22 Fed. Prob. 30 (1958).

efforts to subject certain sorts of human behavior to penal regulation and the persistence of police corruption and abuse of power?[8] Studies of public attitudes toward other sorts of criminal legislation might provide valuable clues as to whether given regulatory objectives are more likely to be attained by the provision of criminal penalties or by other kinds of legal sanctions. It ought to be re-emphasized that the question, What sorts of behavior should be declared criminal? is one to which the behavioral sciences might contribute vital insights. This they have largely failed to do, and we are the poorer for it.

Another example of the narrowing of interests that has accompanied the rise of the rehabilitative ideal is the lack of concern with the idea of deterrence—indeed many modern criminologists are hostile toward it.[9] This, again, is a most surprising development. It must surely be apparent that the criminal law has a general preventive function to perform in the interests of public order and of security of life, limb, and possessions. Indeed, there is reason to assert that the influence of criminal sanctions on the millions who never engage in serious criminality is of greater social importance than their impact on the hundreds of thousands who do. Certainly, the assumptions of those who make our laws is that the denouncing of certain kinds of conduct as criminal and providing the means for the enforcement of legislative prohibitions will generally prevent or minimize

[8] An interesting question of this kind has recently been debated in England centering on the proposals for enhanced penalties for prostitution offenses made in the recently issued Wolfenden Report. See Fairfield, *Notes on Prostitution*, 9 BRIT. J. DELIN. 164, 173 (1959).

[9] But see Andenaes, *General Prevention—Illusion or Reality?* 43 J. CRIM. L., C. & P.S. 176 (1952).

such behavior. Just what the precise mechanisms of deterrence are is not well understood. Perhaps it results, on occasion, from the naked threat of punishment. Perhaps, more frequently, it derives from a more subtle process wherein the mores and moral sense of the community are recruited to advance the attainment of the criminal law's objectives. The point is that we know very little about these vital matters, and the resources of the behavioral sciences have rarely been employed to contribute knowledge and insight in their investigation. Not only have the criminologists displayed little interest in these matters, some have suggested that the whole idea of general prevention is invalid or worse. Thus, speaking of the deterrent theory of punishment, the authors of a leading textbook in criminology assert: "This is simply a derived rationalization of revenge. Though social revenge is the actual psychological basis of punishment today, the apologists for the punitive regime are likely to bring forward in their defense the more sophisticated, but equally futile, contention that punishment deters from [*sic*] crime."[10] We are thus confronted by a situation in which the dominance of the rehabilitative ideal not only diverts attention from many serious issues but leads to a denial that these issues even exist.

DEBASEMENT OF THE REHABILITATIVE IDEAL

I now turn to another kind of difficulty that has accompanied the rise of the rehabilitative ideal in the areas of corrections and criminal justice. It is a familiar observation that

[10] BARNES & TEETERS, NEW HORIZONS IN CRIMINOLOGY 337 (2d ed. 1954). The context in which these statements appear also deserves attention.

an idea once propagated and introduced into the active affairs of life undergoes change. The real significance of an idea as it evolves in actual practice may be quite different from that intended by those who conceived it and gave it initial support. An idea tends to lead a life of its own; and modern history is full of the unintended consequences of seminal ideas. The application of the rehabilitative ideal to the institutions of criminal justice presents a striking example of such a development. My second proposition, then, is that the rehabilitative ideal has been debased in practice and that the consequences resulting from this debasement are serious and, at times, dangerous.

This proposition may be supported, first, by the observation that, under the dominance of the rehabilitative ideal, the language of therapy is frequently employed, wittingly or unwittingly, to disguise the true state of affairs that prevails in our custodial institutions and at other points in the correctional process. Certain measures, like the sexual psychopath laws, have been advanced and supported as therapeutic in nature when, in fact, such a characterization seems highly dubious.[11] Too often the vocabulary of therapy has been exploited to serve a public-relations function. Recently, I visited an institution devoted to the diagnosis and treatment of disturbed children. The institution had been established with high hopes and, for once, with the enthusiastic support of the state legislature. Nevertheless, fifty minutes of an hour's lecture, delivered by a supervising psychiatrist before we toured the building, were devoted to custodial problems. This fixation on problems of custody was reflected in the institutional arrangements which included, under a properly

[11] See discussion pp. 14–15 *supra*.

euphemistic label, a cell for solitary confinement.[12] Even more disturbing was the tendency of the staff to justify these custodial measures in therapeutic terms. Perhaps on occasion the requirements of institutional security and treatment coincide. But the inducements to self-deception in such situations are strong and all too apparent. In short, the language of therapy has frequently provided a formidable obstacle to a realistic analysis of the conditions that confront us. And realism in considering these problems is the one quality that we require above all others.[13]

There is a second kind of unintended consequence that results from the application of the rehabilitative ideal to the practical administration of criminal justice. Surprisingly enough, the rehabilitative ideal has often led to increased severity of penal measures. This tendency may be seen in the operation of the juvenile court. Although frequently condemned by the popular press as a device for leniency, the juvenile court is authorized to intervene punitively in many situations in which the conduct, were it committed by an adult, would be wholly ignored by the law or would subject the adult to the mildest of sanctions. The tendency of proposals for wholly indeterminate sentences, a clearly identifiable fruit of the rehabilitative ideal, is unmistakably in the

[12] As I recall, it was referred to as the "quiet room." In another institution the boy was required to stand before a wall while a seventy pound fire hose was played on his back. This procedure went under name of "hydrotherapy."

[13] *Cf.* Wechsler, *Law, Morals, and Psychiatry,* 18 COLUM. L. SCHOOL NEWS 2, 4 (1959) : "The danger rather is that coercive regimes we would not sanction in the name of punishment or of correction will be sanctified in the name of therapy without providing the resources for a therapeutic operation."

direction of lengthened periods of imprisonment.[14] A large variety of statutes authorizing what is called "civil" commitment of persons, but which, except for the reduced protections afforded the parties proceeded against, are essentially criminal in nature, provide for absolutely indeterminate periods of confinement. Experience has demonstrated that, in practice, there is a strong tendency for the rehabilitative ideal to serve purposes that are essentially incapacitative rather than therapeutic in character.[15]

THE REHABILITATIVE IDEAL AND INDIVIDUAL LIBERTY

This reference to the tendency of the rehabilitative ideal to encourage increasingly long periods of incarceration brings me to my final proposition. It is that the rise of the rehabilitative ideal has often been accompanied by attitudes and measures that conflict, sometimes seriously, with the values of individual liberty and volition. As I have already observed, the role of the behavioral sciences in the administration of criminal justice and in the areas of public policy lying on the borderland of the criminal law is one of obvious importance. But I suggest that, if the function of criminal justice is considered in its proper dimensions, it will be discovered that the most fundamental problems in these areas are not those of psychiatry, sociology, social case work, or social psychology. On the contrary, the most fundamental problems are those of political philosophy and po-

[14] *Cf.* Tappan, *Sentencing under the Model Penal Code*, 23 LAW & CONTEMP. PROB. 528, 530 (1958).

[15] *Cf.* HALL, GENERAL PRINCIPLES OF CRIMINAL LAW 551 (1947). And see SELLIN, THE PROTECTIVE CODE: A SWEDISH PROPOSAL 9 (1957).

litical science. The administration of the criminal law presents to any community the most extreme issues of the proper relations of the individual citizen to state power. We are concerned here with the perennial issue of political authority: Under what circumstances is the state justified in bringing its force to bear on the individual human being? These issues, of course, are not confined to the criminal law, but it is in the area of penal regulation that they are most dramatically manifested. The criminal law, then, is located somewhere near the center of the political problem, as the history of the twentieth century abundantly reveals. It is no accident, after all, that the agencies of criminal justice and law enforcement are those first seized by an emerging totalitarian regime.[16] In short, a study of criminal justice is fundamentally a study in the exercise of political power. No such study can properly avoid the problem of the abuse of power.

The obligation of containing power within the limits suggested by a community's political values has been considerably complicated by the rise of the rehabilitative ideal. For the problem today is one of regulating the exercise of power by men of good will, whose motivations are to help not to injure, and whose ambitions are quite different from those of the political adventurer so familiar to history. There is a tendency for such persons to claim immunity from the usual forms of restraint and to insist that professionalism and a devotion to science provide sufficient protection against unwarranted invasion of individual rights. This attitude is subjected to mordant criticism by Aldous Huxley in his book, *Brave New World Revisited*. Mr. Huxley observes: "There

[16] This development in the case of Germany may be gleaned from CRANKSHAW, GESTAPO (1956).

seems to be a touching belief among certain Ph.D's in sociology that Ph.D's in sociology will never be corrupted by power. Like Sir Galahad's, their strength is the strength of ten because their heart is pure—and their heart is pure because they are scientists and have taken six thousand hours of social studies."[17] I suspect that Mr. Huxley would have been willing to extend his point to include professional groups other than the sociologists. There is one proposition which, if generally understood, would contribute more to clear thinking on these matters than any other. It is not a new insight. Garofalo, asserted: "The mere deprivation of liberty, however benign the administration of the place of confinement, is undeniably punishment."[18] This proposition may be rephrased as follows: Measures which subject individuals to the substantial and involuntary deprivation of their liberty contain an inescapable punitive element, and this reality is not altered by the facts that the motivations that prompt incarceration are to provide therapy or otherwise contribute to the person's well-being or reform. As such, these measures must be closely scrutinized to insure that power is being applied consistently with those values of the community that justify interference with liberty for only the most clear and compelling reasons.

But the point I am making requires more specific and concrete application to be entirely meaningful. It should be pointed out, first, that the values of individual liberty may be imperiled by claims to knowledge and therapeutic technique that we, in fact, do not possess and by our failure to concede candidly what we do not know. At times, practitioners of the behavioral sciences have been guilty of these

[17] Huxley, Brave New World Revisited 34–35 (1958).

[18] Garofalo, Criminology 241–42 (Millar transl. 1914).

faults. At other times, such errors have supplied the assumptions on which legislators, lawyers, and lay people generally have proceeded. An illustration of these dangers is provided by the sexual psychopath laws, to which I return, for they epitomize admirably some of the worst tendencies of modern practice.[19] Doubts almost as serious can be raised as to a whole range of other measures. The laws providing for the commitment of persons displaying the classic symptoms of psychosis and advanced mental disorder have proved a seductive analogy for other proposals. But does our knowledge of human behavior really justify the extension of these measures to provide for the indefinite commitment of persons otherwise afflicted?

There are other ways in which the modern tendencies of thought accompanying the rise of the rehabilitative ideal have imperiled basic political values. The most important of these is the encouragement of procedural laxness and irregularity. It is my impression that there is a greater awareness of these dangers today than at some other times in the past. Nevertheless, in our courts of so-called socialized justice one may still observe, on occasion, a tendency to assume that, since the purpose of the proceeding is to "help" rather than to "punish," some lack of concern in establishing the charges against the person before the court may be justified. Thus, in some courts the judge is supplied with a report on the offender by the psychiatric clinic before the judgment of guilt or acquittal is announced. Such reports, while they may be relevant to the defendant's need for therapy or confinement, are ordinarily wholly irrelevant to the issue of his guilt of the particular offense charged. Yet it asks too much of human nature to assume that the judge is

[19] See discussion pp. 14–15 *supra*.

never influenced on the issue of guilt or innocence by a strongly adverse psychiatric report.

Let me give one final illustration of the problems that have accompanied the rise of the rehabilitative ideal. Some time ago we encountered a man in his eighties incarcerated in a state institution. He had been confined for some thirty years under a statute calling for the automatic commitment of defendants acquitted on grounds of insanity in criminal trials. It was generally agreed by the institution's personnel that he was not then psychotic and probably had never been psychotic. The fact seemed to be that he had killed his wife while drunk. An elderly sister of the old man was able and willing to provide him with a home, and he was understandably eager to leave the institution. When we asked the director of the institution why the old man was not released, he gave two significant answers. In the first place, he said, the statute requires me to find that this inmate is no longer a danger to the community; this I cannot do, for he may kill again. And of course the director was right. However unlikely commission of homicide by such a man in his eighties might appear, the director could not be certain. But, as far as that goes, he could not be certain also about himself or about you or me. The second answer was equally interesting. The old man, he said, is better off here. To understand the full significance of this reply it is necessary to know something about the place of confinement. Although called a hospital, it was in fact a prison, and not at all a progressive prison. Nothing worthy of the name of therapy was provided and very little even by way of recreational facilities.

This case points several morals. It illustrates, first, a failure of the law to deal adequately with the new requirements which are being placed upon it. The statute, as a condition of the release of the inmate, required the director of the institution virtually to warrant the future good behavior of the inmate, and, in so doing, made unrealistic and impossible demands on expert judgment. This might be remedied by the formulation of release criteria more consonant with actuality. Provisions for conditional release to test the inmate's reaction to the free community would considerably reduce the strain on administrative decision-making. But there is more here. Perhaps the case reflects that arrogance and insensitivity to human values to which men who have no reason to doubt their own motives appear peculiarly susceptible.[20]

I have attempted to describe some of the continuing problems and difficulties associated with, what I have called, the rise of the rehabilitative ideal. In so doing, I have not sought to cast doubt on the substantial benefits associated with that movement. It has exposed some of the most intractable problems of our time to the solvent properties of human intelligence. Moreover, the devotion to the ideal of empirical investigation provides the movement with a self-correcting mechanism of great importance and justifies hopes for constructive future development.

[20] Another remarkable example is provided by the case, In re Maddox, 351 Mich. 358, 88 N.W.2d 470 (1958). Professor Wechsler, *op. cit. supra* note 13, at 4, describes the facts and holding as follows: "Only the other day, the Supreme Court of Michigan ordered the release of a prisoner in their State prison at Jackson, who had been transferred from the Ionia State Hospital to which he was committed as a psychopath. The ground of transfer, which was defended seriously by a State psychiatrist, was that the prisoner was 'adamant' in refusing to admit sexual deviation that was the basis of his commitment; and thus, in the psychiatrist's view, resistant to therapy. The Court's answer was, of course, that he had not been tried for an offense."

Nevertheless, no intellectual movement produces only un-mixed blessings. I have suggested that the ascendency of the rehabilitative ideal has, as one of its unfortunate conse-quences, diverted attention from other questions of great criminological importance. This has operated unfavorably to the full development of criminological science. Not only is this true, but the failure of many students and practition-ers in the relevant areas to concern themselves with the full context of criminal justice has produced measures danger-ous to basic political values and has, on occasion, encour-aged the debasement of the rehabilitative ideal to produce results which are unsupportable whether measured by the objectives of therapy or of correction. The worst manifesta-tions of these tendencies are undoubtedly deplored as sin-cerely by competent therapists as by others. But the occur-rences are neither so infrequent nor so trivial that they can be safely ignored.

THE JUVENILE COURT AND THE
LIMITS OF JUVENILE JUSTICE

The years since World War II have brought about a revival
of interest in the American juvenile court. Following the
burst of enthusiasm in the early years of the century that
led to widespread adoption of juvenile court legislation, the
institution in many localities suffered the consequences of
public apathy and neglect. This neglect and its consequences
are still being felt; but in recent years the court has again
become the subject of discussion and debate, and this to a
degree not approached for a half-century. Not all supporters
of the juvenile court movement have welcomed the new attention, for some modern critics have subjected basic assumptions of the movement to challenge and doubt. Fortu-
nately, however, most persons who wish well for the court
recognize the recent discussion as a source of strength. Indeed, unless one assumes that the little band of creative
reformers who launched the juvenile court at the turn of the
century was possessed of revealed truth, final and unassail-
able, it must be recognized that criticism and analysis are

Delivered as a lecture at Wayne State University, Detroit, Mich-
igan, on March 13, 1963, in a series jointly sponsored by the Law
School and the Delinquency Control Training Center of Wayne
State University.

essential to the proper evolution of the institution and its adaptation to current realities.

The modern reappraisal of the juvenile court, however, has not proceeded far. We have only begun to make use of the techniques and insights that have been acquired in the study of other social institutions.[1] We are only beginning to obtain systematic information on what, in reality, the juvenile court is and does. Certainly we are far from formulating secure principles to direct its future development. These are formidable tasks and require more thought and effort than have thus far been devoted to them, even in this period of increasing interest in the court and its functions.

The juvenile court, both in theory and practice, is an institution of remarkable complexity. It is called upon to perform a bewildering variety of functions. On the one hand, it administers what are essentially welfare functions, such as the exercise of its dependency jurisdiction. On the other hand, it may be required to provide a forum for criminal prosecution, as in cases of adults alleged to have contributed to the delinquency of minors. The juvenile court is a court; but it is also a governmental agency charged with manifold administrative responsibilities and, in some localities, the performance of clinical services. Not only does the court perform a variety of functions and assume a variety of roles, it must inevitably express a wide range of values and aspirations. But functions conflict and values collide; hence, there must be some sort of mediation or accommodation of the various goals and values if the institution is to function

[1] Compare examples of "organizational analysis" as applied to prisons and other custodial institutions: CLEMMER, THE PRISON COMMUNITY (1940); SYKES, THE SOCIETY OF CAPTIVES (1958); SOCIAL SCIENCE RESEARCH COUNCIL, THEORETICAL STUDIES OF SOCIAL ORGANIZATION OF THE PRISON (Pamphlet 15, 1960).

at all. This accommodation and compromise may result from intelligent deliberation or it may be the product of caprice and indifference.

But the complexity which obstructs understanding and reappraisal of the juvenile court involves more than the proliferation of functions or the conflict of conscious goals and values. We have come to realize that understanding an institution requires that we know more than the motives and aspirations of those who created it and of those who operate it. In the language of Merton, we must be concerned not only with its manifest functions but with its latent functions;[2] not only with what the institution consciously attempts to do but with what it does in fact. And we may expect to discover in looking closely at the juvenile court that its operations result in certain unintended and unanticipated consequences, consequences no less real because they are unintended and unanticipated.

In short, it is clear that wisdom and understanding in this area cannot be purchased cheaply. The inquiry and critical analysis required demand the contributions of many disciplines and much time, ingenuity, and resources. They also demand a willingness to subject cherished presuppositions to the hazards of inquiry and analysis. This is not to deny that there are short-term goals of practical reform worthy of support; but it is to suggest that our fundamental need is knowledge and understanding. Accordingly, I am concerned less with the immediate reform of the juvenile court and more with a few general questions which, it has seemed to me, may have some relevance to a modern reconsideration of the court.

Perhaps the search for understanding can best begin with

[2] MERTON, SOCIAL THEORY AND SOCIAL STRUCTURE 60–64 (rev. ed. 1957).

a consideration of the history and antecedents of the juvenile court movement. No institution as complex as the juvenile court emerges suddenly and fully formed. On the contrary, the juvenile court can properly be regarded as the culmination of certain ideas and tendencies of thought that had their origins at least as early as the eighteenth-century Enlightenment. Throughout the century that followed many of these distinctive ideas were given practical application, so that by the time the first juvenile court legislation became effective in Illinois on July 1, 1899, many of its assumptions were familiar and well tested. Thus the nineteenth century saw the beginnings of the effort to segregate juveniles from adult offenders in detention and correctional institutions and the establishment of cottage-type schools for children. Separate courts or divisions of courts for children were put into operation in several localities, and systems of probation were devised and administered.[3] These reforms were part of a broader effort to advance the welfare of children, evidenced both in the United States and western Europe, which included the rise of public education, the development of protective services for dependent and neglected children, and agitation against child labor and other abuses of children in industry. All these activities were in some degree influenced by new theories of human behavior which sometimes challenged the validity of such basic concepts of the legal order as the concept of criminal responsibility and resulted, among other things, in the formation of the schools of positivist criminology.[4]

[3] See Caldwell, *The Juvenile Court: Its Development and Some Major Problems,* 51 J. CRIM. L., C. & P. S. 493 (1961) ; Rosenheim, *Perennial Problems in the Juvenile Court,* in JUSTICE FOR THE CHILD 1–16 (Rosenheim ed. 1962).

[4] Consult Jeffery, *The Historical Development of Criminology,* in PIONEERS IN CRIMINOLOGY 364 *et seq.* (Mannheim ed. 1960).

It is never possible to explain completely the rise of an elaborate system of thought and practice such as that given expression in the juvenile court movement. But most social movements can be understood, in part, as reactions against older modes of thought and practice. There is no doubt that the juvenile court represents to a significant degree a reaction against the older methods of dealing with children which were employed by the legal order. That some of these methods were and are properly the subject of protest is also clear. Historical examples of the inhumanity of criminal justice in confronting the problem of the misbehaving child and the insensitivity of public attitudes that supported these practices still possess the power to shock and startle. Thus, in the first half of the last century the diarist, Charles Grenville, in describing a hanging at Tyburn gaol, expressed astonishment at the incomprehensible attitude of the boys about to be hanged. "Never," he is reported as saying, "did I see boys cry so."[5] But the demonstration that the old days were in many respects the bad old days does not depend upon the collection of historical examples. The badness of much of the older practices is demonstrated by such as have persisted to the present day. For at least two centuries thoughtful persons have recognized the danger of detaining juveniles in facilities that bring them into contact with older offenders. And yet, in many parts of the country our detention practices have not taken this small first step in the direction of decency and rationality.[6] At the adult level, American corrections have rarely been capable of making the elementary distinction between the accused person charged with crime and the convicted offender.

[5] Quoted in BEVAN, IN PLACE OF FEAR 177 (1952).

[6] See, *e.g.*, Norman, *The Detention Home*, 241 Annals 161 (January, 1949).

In most of our jails both classes of persons are indiscriminately confined together and subjected to basically the same regimen.[7] We know that many of the old ways are bad ways because we can observe their effects in present practice; we are able thereby to gain some appreciation of the intensity of the reaction which is expressed in efforts at reform like the juvenile court movement.

The juvenile court may thus be regarded as a response to problems that are real and important. There is no doubt that the juvenile court movement was founded on strong and explicit dissatisfaction with conditions then generally prevailing and was intended to effect a radical and thorough-going reform. Not only were conditions in juvenile custodial institutions to be improved, but separate and distinctive judicial proceedings were to be established and the benefits of probation services to be extended. A whole new view of juvenile misbehavior as essentially non-criminal was propounded and a completely non-punitive course of treatment was to be substituted for the old criminal sanctions. Writing in 1909, Judge Julian Mack described the ideal and responsibility of the juvenile court in the following terms: ". . . to find out what [the child] is, physically, mentally, morally, and then if it learns that he is treading the path that leads to criminality, to take him in charge, not so much to punish as to reform, not to degrade but to uplift, not to crush but to develop, not to make him a criminal but a worthy citizen."[8] The juvenile court thus

[7] See Foote, *Forward: Comment on the New York Bail Study*, 106 U. PA. L. REV. 685, 689 (1958). And note the comments in chapter 3 of the ATTORNEY GENERAL'S COMMITTEE ON POVERTY AND THE ADMINISTRATION OF FEDERAL CRIMINAL JUSTICE REP. (1963).

[8] Mack, *The Juvenile Court*, 23 HARV. L. REV. 104, 107 (1909).

represents the most important and ambitious effort yet undertaken by our law to give practical expression to the rehabilitative ideal.

It reveals, I believe, no hostility toward the rehabilitative ideal to suggest that the effort to give it expression is attended by certain distinctive problems and that the tendency to view the court in exclusively rehabilitative or therapeutic terms imposes its own characteristic limitations. Nor should this be regarded as surprising. We are not blessed with a capacity to view human problems in all their infinite complexities, and any posture assumed in the presence of large social issues is likely to express its own particular bias and be vulnerable to its own forms of pathology. In reacting against old errors we are constantly in danger of being enslaved by our emancipation. This is not to say that progress is impossible because we are doomed simply to exchange old errors for new. It is to say that in the process of reform we may encounter new and distinctive problems. To insure that progress will result from reform, we must be continually vigilant in order to detect the unanticipated consequences of our action.

With these matters in mind we may now inquire whether the concept of the juvenile court as expressed by its founders and frequently repeated in various forms of language by later proponents provides a theory adequate to describe what the court is and to define what its role ought to be now and in the future. In his eloquent essay entitled "Philosophy of the Juvenile Court," the late Judge Schramm of Pittsburgh, remarked: "Juvenile courts are the least understood and the most misunderstood of the courts of our land."[9] Anyone who has observed the juvenile court over

[9] Schramm, *Philosophy of the Juvenile Court,* 241 Annals 101 (January, 1949).

any considerable period of time has sensed, on occasion, a tension between the court and the community. Most supporters of the court are disposed to explain this tension by the persistence of an impulse for retribution in the public at large and by a lack of whole-hearted commitment to the rehabilitative ideal. It would be difficult to deny that this explanation contains a large element of truth. But is it a complete and adequate explanation? The tension to which I refer is sometimes made explicit in the juvenile court legislation itself. In the first section of the Michigan juvenile court act, the legislature declared that the law should be liberally construed so as to advance "the child's welfare and the best interest of the state."[10] Are these objectives in all cases the same? Are there instances in which the best interests of the community, if not inconsistent with the welfare of the child, are at least to some degree separate and distinct? Is it possible that the traditional view of the court as exclusively or largely a therapeutic or rehabilitative agency has obstructed identification of areas of legitimate community interest that the court may properly be expected to serve? These are large and difficult questions, and the remarks that follow represent only a tentative effort to explore the issues as they relate to the court's delinquency jurisdiction.

The typical, indeed almost automatic, reaction to the issues posed, on the part of those imbued with the classic theory of the court, is to deny the possibility of any community interest separate from, and certainly any community interest adverse to, the welfare of the child brought before the juvenile court. If, it is argued, we are able to provide the delinquent child with therapy and treatment

[10] MICH. COMP. LAWS §712 A.1 (1948).

that will profoundly change his motivations and behavior so that in the future he will be able and disposed to live in harmony, rather than at war, with the community, we shall not only have advanced the welfare of the child but at the same time have made a most fundamental contribution to the "interest of the state." That this response has genuine force and cogency ought to be recognized. A community which fails simply for want of vision or energy to provide its children with the means of therapy and rehabilitation will inevitably suffer the effects of self-inflicted wounds. Moreover, this response gives expression to an aspiration and an ideal that have supplied the impetus for much of the juvenile court's soundest achievement. And yet, it must be concluded by those seeking understanding of the court that the response is insufficient. We still need to inquire whether, assuming full capability to achieve the objectives of rehabilitation, the court has purposes to serve that involve more than the interests and welfare of the particular children coming before it. We need also to inquire about the purposes of the court in those cases in which the court is incapable of achieving its rehabilitative objectives, either because of the limits of scientific knowledge or because of the inadequacies of the facilities and personnel available to it or because the particular problems of adolescent misconduct are of the sort that give rise to issues no court can adequately confront or resolve.

It is the point last mentioned which perhaps best exposes the inadequacy of any theory of the juvenile court that views the institution wholly as a therapeutic or rehabilitative device. For it is an unfortunate fact that the juvenile court of every large urban community is confronted by significant numbers of adolescents whose behavior cannot be ignored because it imperils the basic security of the community, and who, as a class, elude the reformative capabilities of the court. These are adolescents who are not mentally ill in any sense of the term that meaningfully distinguishes this group of young persons from the population as a whole. On the contrary, these are children alienated from the legitimate institutions of society, lacking in opportunities for employment and goal satisfactions, victims of discrimination and cultural deprivation. The behavior of such children, even that which contributes most to community concern and insecurity, may often reflect normal adaptation to the conditions of life to which they are subjected. Some modern writers have suggested that much violent group behavior on the part of adolescents reflects an effort to obtain prestige or to force themselves onto the attention of the community.[11] However this may be, it appears clear that such behavior is in some measure the product of conditions not within the control of the court, conditions which create the environment to which the child must return after the program of treatment instituted by the juvenile court has come to an end.

There is surely nothing new in this statement. It constitutes no revelation to anyone acquainted with the operations of the American juvenile court to be told that it is regularly required to act in cases of children whose prognosis for rehabilitation at the hands of the court is highly unfavorable. What are the implications of this observation? Surely not that such cases should be excluded from the jurisdiction of the juvenile court; for the processes of the court, with all their limitations, may still represent the best

[11] See, *e.g.*, CLOWARD & OHLIN, DELINQUENCY AND OPPORTUNITY (1960).

and least harmful method that our civilization has devised to handle these problems. But it is, in my judgment, both inaccurate and deceptive to describe the operation of the juvenile court in this area as the exercise of a rehabilitative or therapeutic function. These cases are being adjudicated by the court for one principal reason: because they involve disturbing and dangerous behavior on the part of adolescents which the community must respond and attend to, for it is behavior that threatens the security and well-being of the community. The primary function being served in these cases, now and for what is likely to be an extended period in the future, is the temporary incapacitation of children found to constitute a threat to the community's interest. In short, the value advanced is not primarily that of the welfare of the child adjudicated a delinquent. This is due not so much to the court's lack of commitment to the rehabilitative ideal as to the incapacity of the court and its instrumentalities to deal effectively with the conditions giving rise to delinquent behavior.

Thus if our concern is to understand what the juvenile court is and what in significant measure it is likely to be in the years ahead, these facts cannot be ignored. In a great many cases the juvenile court must perform functions essentially similar to those exercised by any court adjudicating cases of persons charged with dangerous and disturbing behavior. It must reassert the norms and standards of the community when confronted by seriously deviant conduct, and it must protect the security of the community by such measures as it has at its disposal, even though the available means may be unsatisfactory when viewed either from the standpoint of the community interest or of the welfare of the delinquent child. These propositions do no more than describe a situation which is familiar to all those who have observed the work of the juvenile court. What is remarkable is how rarely such observations have been included in what might be called the "official" literature of the court.

It may be objected, of course, that the theory of the court ought to emphasize those elements that distinguish it from, rather than identify it with, other agencies of justice. Moreover, the rehabilitative ideal, the aspiration to advance "the best interests of the child," has provided impetus and inspiration for the important effort to improve and render more rational our methods of dealing with children who have run afoul of the community's standards and expectations. The importance of preserving the ideal and invigorating the dynamics of reform cannot, I believe, be seriously doubted. Yet this does not justify a refusal to recognize candidly the realities that confront us. Theory is important because, among other reasons, it affects our conduct; a theory that is partial and incomplete is likely to produce unsatisfactory results. Insofar as the juvenile court is concerned, the bad results of inadequate theory are not merely a matter of speculation and conjecture. They are tangible and can be readily identified.

First, the failure to perceive that the juvenile court is often called upon to protect the community from acts of violence or depredations of property and to do this by the use of means that may in no sense advance the welfare of the delinquent child has, on occasion, encouraged laxness and unfairness in the procedures employed by the court in executing its charging, adjudicatory, and dispositional functions. Even today many persons professionally involved in the processes of juvenile justice conceive of the court as a large welfare agency blessed by some mysterious gift of

Providence with access to the coercive powers of the state.
Various factors combine to strengthen this impression.
These include a widespread failure to communicate to members of the court's social staff the legal presuppositions of
the system, the fact that the court deals with many matters
that are essentially of a welfare character, and the circumstance that some juvenile court legislation, particularly the
older statutes, defines the delinquency concept in terms so
vague and flexible as to allow an assertion of jurisdiction
in almost any case in which the intervention of the court
is thought to be helpful to the child.[12] Nevertheless, the
jurisdictional principle on which the court properly proceeds in the delinquency area is, not the presumed ability
of the court to be of service to the particular child, but the
existence of behavior on the part of the child that is dangerous to the community's security or that imminently
threatens such danger. Since the intervention of the court
can only be justified by the existence of certain behavioral
facts, it is of the highest importance that the procedures of
notice and adjudication be adapted to careful and reliable
fact-finding. Fair and reliable fact-finding procedures are,
of course, essential in all cases, including those in which
the court's disposition of the case may be expected to result
in a genuine rehabilitative effort. But the importance of fair
procedures may be more readily perceived when it is noted
that in many delinquency proceedings the rehabilitative effort is at best a matter of secondary concern and that the
juvenile court is performing a function in many respects

[12] An interesting discussion of related problems may be found in
Paulsen, *The Delinquency, Neglect, and Dependency Jurisdiction
of the Juvenile Court*, in JUSTICE FOR THE CHILD 44 *et seq*. (Rosenheim ed. 1962).

similar to that of courts of criminal justice. This surely suggests that the essence, if not the precise content, of the fair procedures required to be provided in other courts should also be respected in the juvenile court. These points warrant further attention; but since the problems of fair procedure in the juvenile courts have been canvassed so frequently in recent years, this limited reference may perhaps be sufficient.[13]

Other difficulties arise from an insufficient conception of the court's role and the court's capabilities. Thus, the tendency to describe the court only by reference to its therapeutic or rehabilitative potential creates the peril of unrealistic and unrealizable expectations. In more than one American locality friends of the juvenile court, particularly when seeking to recruit larger financial support from the public, have advanced insupportable claims as to the court's capabilities in the control of juvenile delinquency through the processes of treatment and supervision of delinquent children. Such claims are rarely, if ever, made with the conscious purpose to deceive. On the contrary, they are born of enthusiasm and devotion, and they reflect the normal human tendency to confuse wish for reality, aspiration for existing fact. Yet one wonders whether in the long run more cautious and responsible public representations might serve better the juvenile court movement. Disillusionment is the product of disappointed expectations; and the resulting public apathy, or even hostility, to the court may obstruct its achieving those goals experience has shown clearly to be within its competence.

But the more serious problems are those that arise from confusion as to the nature of the court and its capabilities

[13] See discussion pp. 16–23 *supra*.

on the part of those directly engaged in the work of the court and those charged with developing a program of care and custody of children brought within the court's jurisdiction. Such confusion militates against sound judgment in determining what the needs of the institution are, assigning priorities, and making proper allocation of limited and often inadequate resources. That the welfare of many delinquent children has been advanced as a result of their contacts with the juvenile court and that more substantial gains in this respect could be made in many localities through more generous governmental support of the court's program are facts that demand acknowledgment in any appraisal of the court and its work. Nevertheless, if one views the processes of American juvenile justice as a whole, one is compelled to conclude that in a broad spectrum of cases the immediate need and the immediate goal are less the rehabilitation or changing of children for the better and more the altering of conditions and practices that render children worse and more dangerous as a result of their contacts with the official agencies. In few localities have we fully achieved the basic objectives of decency and humanity in dealing with the misbehaving child. The attainment of these objectives, although sometimes obstructed by formidable difficulties, is surely not impossible. One difficulty may be that our larger ambitions may sometimes divert us and prevent us from achieving the more modest goals. Perhaps this phenomenon can be illustrated by a concrete example. Several years ago the legislature of an American state established at considerable expense a diagnostic center for children committed by the juvenile courts of the state. An elaborate facility was erected and manned. The children were subjected to interviews and batteries of tests before being assigned to the state training schools. Inquiry soon revealed, however, that the intensive programs of thearapy and treatment recommended for the children by personnel of the diagnostic center were being largely ignored in the training schools, and this for the very good reason that the training schools lacked the facilities and skills essential to carry the recommendations into effect. To my knowledge, the situation has not materially changed in the intervening years. This incident is, of course, by no means unique, and it demonstrates that the ambition to achieve, or appear to achieve, important therapeutic objectives may on occasion distort judgment and a sense of priorities. For in the case described, however valuable the diagnostic center may one day prove to be, it is clear that it was established at the expense of less spectacular measures—measures urgently required to advance the rationality and decency of the system. These measures included such mundane matters as the improvement of the physical environment of the training schools and the enhancement of the quality of institutional programs of academic and vocational instruction.

One other set of problems arising from inaccurate or mistaken conceptions of the court's roles and capabilities should be mentioned. These relate to the nature and extent of the contribution the court may be expected to make to the solution of the larger problems of delinquency prevention and control. Whatever may have been the hopes of early supporters of the juvenile court movement, there must surely be few persons today who fail to recognize that effective confrontation of seriously disturbing adolescent behavior requires much more by way of techniques and resources than the court alone can command or provide. Since, however, the juvenile court presumably has a contribution to make, one of the most pressing modern concerns has come to be that of defining the role of the court in relation to other community agencies and programs aimed at minimizing serious juvenile misconduct. It is no more than just to say that progress in this respect has not been impressive. Indeed, the typical situation, even in communities in which the problems of delinquency are most urgent, is one in which the efforts of the various interested agencies are almost wholly unco-ordinated, with the result that the efforts of one agency not only do not gain strength and support from those of other agencies but may sometimes be frustrated and rendered largely ineffectual by the efforts of other agencies. The complexities here are almost infinite; but it must be apparent that sound integration of the court's efforts into community programs of delinquency prevention and control must be preceded by a realistic appraisal of the court's role and its capacity to make effective contributions to a total effort.

Until events provide a basis for more sanguine hopes, however, a healthy skepticism seems appropriate. Although the various functions of the juvenile court are important and are, in fact, indispensable, and even though a significantly large fraction of the nation's adolescent population makes contact each year with the juvenile court,[14] it seems likely that the court's contributions to the eradication of delinquency will be limited and peripheral. Indeed, insofar as the delinquency phenomenon is associated with

[14] "The United States Children's Bureau has estimated that as many as 12 per cent of all American youth—and roughly 20 per cent of all our country's boys—will be referred to juvenile courts on delinquency charges at some time between the ages of ten and seventeen." Shireman, *Foreword* in Rosenheim, *op. cit. supra* note 12, at v.

patterns of life in the subcultures of our large cities, it may be doubted whether fundamental gains can be achieved by any program directed to ends more limited than the radical alteration of the patterns of life that prevail in such areas. If this be true (and no assertions on this subject can confidently be offered), fundamental solutions appear to lie in the direction of integrating our alienated populations into full participation in the social, economic, political, and cultural life of our communities. The difficulties involved hardly need to be itemized, for such measures run afoul of the interests, attitudes, and prejudices of the dominant segments of our population. It is precisely at this point that the juvenile court may provide an obstacle to fundamental reform unless great care is taken. For it may be true that the tendency to attribute capabilities to the court that it does not possess represents in some degree a largely unpremeditated effort to evade the necessity of accepting more fundamental and less comfortable alternatives. Surely we shall be confronted by the ultimate irony if the juvenile court, itself the product of a radical and creative movement of reform, should today be permitted to serve as an obstruction to the basic reforms required in mid-twentieth-century America.

I have attempted to suggest and demonstrate that a full and accurate conception of the work of the juvenile court and its potential is of the greatest importance to its proper functioning and to its future development. In suggesting that traditional conceptions of the court are deficient in certain important respects, I have not challenged the importance of the rehabilitative ideal that has played such a vital role in the court's history and development. The court has contributed significantly to the welfare of children and its capacities in this respect have never been fully exploited. Moreover, the court and its allied institutions provide valuable laboratories for acquiring new knowledge and the testing of new rehabilitative techniques. The court, however, is not simply a laboratory or a clinic and the tendency to conceive of it in these terms, largely to the exclusion of the other functions it is called upon to perform, contributes neither to a sound understanding of the institution nor to its proper use in serving the public interest. Self-knowledge is as vital to the proper growth of institutions as it is to the moral and intellectual development of individuals. The perils to sound development are also similar. We need the capacity to distinguish between wish and reality and to determine with reasonable accuracy the limits of our powers and capabilities. Given these capacities, the juvenile court may long extend its useful career and reach levels of achievement not yet attained.

GAROFALO'S CRIMINOLOGY AND
SOME MODERN PROBLEMS

For good reason it is customary to identify Raffaele Garofalo as one of the three leading exponents of the Italian
school of criminology which came into being during the
closing years of the nineteenth century. The relationship
with Lombroso and Ferri is clear, but it ought not to obscure the distinctive quality of Garofalo's thought or the
particular range of his major interests.[1] No doubt the emphasis of his work was in large measure the product of his
distinguished professional career. Born a member of the
Italian nobility in Naples in 1852, he served in his mature
years as a lawyer, prosecutor, and magistrate. In addition,
he performed the duties of a professor of criminal law and

This article originally appeared in 45 J. Crim. L., C. & P.S. 373–
90 (1954) and was reprinted in Pioneers in Criminology (Mannheim ed. 1960). Reprinted here by permission.

[1] *Cf.* De Quiros, Modern Theories of Criminality 28 (De Salvio
transl. 1911): "With the anthropologist Lombroso, the sociologist
Ferri, and the jurisconsult Garofalo, the school of criminal anthropology can be considered as fully established. Hence, one of its
critics has called these three men *evangelists* and their works
gospels. From that time on they are always mentioned in a kind of
trinity, a little divided at times only by Garofalo's political and
penal conservatism."

procedure in the university of his native city. But for whatever cause, there is exhibited in Garofalo's writings a consistent concern with practical reform of the criminal law and legal institutions associated with the administration of criminal justice. This, of course, is not to say that Garofalo's inquiries failed to encompass matters of theoretical scientific interest. But even when he deals with such topics, he displays a continuing effort to relate the fruits of such investigation to the legal context and to gain insights which may be useful in the practical business of legislation and administration. This note is struck in the first paragraph of his *Criminology*. Speaking of the then recent efforts at a scientific study of criminality, he observes: "But when we come to consider how this theory may be applied to legislation, serious difficulties are encountered."[2] Later, discussing Ferri's classification of criminal types, he concludes: "Being of no avail to legislation it is consequently without practical interest."[3] It is perhaps not too much to say that this detailed concern with the concrete problems of legal and institutional reform provides the chief source of interest in Garofalo's writings for most modern readers.

Although Garofalo enjoyed a long and productive scholarly career, he is known principally in this country through his major work, the *Criminology*. The first edition of the book appeared in 1885 when Garofalo was only thirty-three years of age. A second Italian edition was published six years later and a French version, prepared personally by Garofalo, received a sufficiently wide response to justify several subsequent editions. The excellent English transla-

[2] GAROFALO, CRIMINOLOGY 3 (Millar transl. 1914). The work will be cited hereinafter as CRIM.

[3] *Id.* at 134.

tion completed in 1914 by the late Professor Robert W. Millar is based largely on the French edition of 1905.

In approaching a study of the *Criminology* it is well that several general considerations be kept in mind. The work in its original version appeared some eighty years ago. Inevitably time has taken its toll. Many of the assumptions and the data upon which these assumptions are based have been placed in serious doubt by subsequent investigations. More fundamentally, the *Criminology* is in a considerable degree a product of certain important intellectual currents which profoundly affected social thought during the last half of the nineteenth century and which have lost much of their power to impress the modern mind and to stir the modern imagination. The pervasive influence of social Darwinism and the speculations of Herbert Spencer are, for example, clearly discernible at almost every stage of Garofalo's argument. For modern tastes there is perhaps a too-easy assumption of the inevitability of moral progress and the benevolence of political power.[4]

But this is far from denying the continuing interest of the work and its considerable relevance to contemporary issues. For the *Criminology* contributes a full measure of significant insights which are often largely independent of the theoretical superstructure on which Garofalo built. Moreover, the essential honesty of his methods and eagerness to discipline his conclusions by a constant reference to facts do much to bridge the years. There is pleasure, too, in following his lively and often closely reasoned argument. It is perilous

[4] Another difficulty might well be mentioned. Many of Garofalo's illustrations and much of his data relate to patterns of criminality then prevailing in southern Italy, Sicily, and Corsica. These patterns, while perhaps not entirely unique, are sufficiently atypical to increase the difficulties of critical evaluation.

to attempt evaluation of a writer's literary style in translation, but the bite of his language emerges clearly enough.
Thus, commenting on certain of Lombroso's work, he states:
"In his later writing the same writer contended that epi-
lepsy is always to be found in the born criminal. This theory
I shall not stop to discuss since the fact is far from being
established. Moreover, it is flatly contradictory of the theory
of atavism, despite Lombroso's efforts to reconcile the two
theories. It seems hardly possible to conceive our first parents as unhappy epileptics."[5]

THE CONCEPT OF "NATURAL CRIME"

The starting point of any criminological system is the de-
limitation and definition of its subject matter. Even with
the passing of the years, these basic and primary issues remain in agitation and controversy. Garofalo rightly saw,
with a clarity not matched by many who came before and
after him, that the prior questions to be resolved center
about the proper formulation of the concept of crime—the
"criminal" presupposes "crime."[6] Thus at the outset he observes that ". . . although the naturalists speak of the *crimi-*

[5] CRIM. 105–6.

[6] *Cf.* FERRI, CRIMINAL SOCIOLOGY 77–78 (Kelly & Lisle transl.
1917) : "Garofalo's definition was, however, an original and happy
attempt, although for my part, as Fioretti had already remarked
and as I have said elsewhere, I do not feel the antecedent necessity
for such a definition. In my opinion, a definition with which meta-
physicians and classical jurists ever love to begin, can on the contrary only be the ultimate synthesis. It should, therefore, come at
the end and not at the beginning of the researches of criminal sociology. And this is not only because the general reasons of the positive method require it; but also because the difficulty raised by
opponents and combatted by Garofalo is not serious."

nal, they have omitted to tell us what they understand by the word *crime.*"[7]

Perhaps partly in reaction to the excesses of the Austinian school, Garofalo sharply rejected as inadequate for scientific purposes the notion that crime may properly be defined as that conduct for which the law has provided penalties and has denominated criminal. This "juridical" conception, it is urged, fails in that it both includes and excludes behavior properly encompassed in a "sociologic notion of crime." For Garofalo only the latter is of concern to the scientific investigator. In giving content to this sociologic notion he formulates one of his most important concepts: the idea of "natural crime." "Natural" he defines as that ". . . which is not conventional, . . . which exists in human society independently of the circumstances and exigencies of a given epoch or the particular views of the law-maker."[8] In short, "natural crime" consists of that conduct which offends the basic moral sentiments of pity (revulsion against the voluntary infliction of suffering on others) and probity (respect for property rights of others). The basic moral sensibilities appear in more or less advanced form in all civilized societies and are, indeed, essential to the coexistence of individuals in society. Hence, the true criminal against whom society must make defense is he who has revealed the absence or deficiency in himself of either or both these essential moral capacities.

In further refining the concept, Garofalo makes clear that he is speaking only of the sentiments of pity and probity as manifested by the average moral sense of the community, which may fall considerably below the level of moral perception attained by the exceptional and superior

[7] Crim. at 3.   [8] *Id.* at 4.

members of the group. Moreover, the truly criminal act must be harmful to society.[9] At first sight, Garofalo's idea of natural crime may appear as a latter-day revival of the *jus gentium*. And, indeed, he believed that for the western European countries, which had arrived at near the same level of cultural development, a true "law of nations" might be formulated in the penal area, as evidenced by his draft of suggested principles for an international penal code.[10] Nevertheless, as he makes clear, the concept of natural crime does not consist of a catalogue of acts which are universally or widely conceived to be criminal. History, chance, and the varying levels of social development have produced great differences in the kinds of overt behavior characterized as crime at various times and places. The uniformity lies rather in the basic altruistic sentiments of mankind; true crime is that conduct which, upon evaluation by the average moral sense of the particular society under consideration, is deemed offensive to those sentiments.

One further point of clarification needs to be stated. Garofalo does not intend to limit offenses recognized by any government to those included in the category of natural crime.

[9] Garofalo summarizes his position in the following manner: "From what has been said . . . , we may conclude that the element of immorality requisite before a harmful act can be regarded as criminal by public opinion, is the injury to so much of the moral sense as is represented by one or the other of the elementary altruistic sentiments of *pity* and *probity*. Moreover, the injury must wound these sentiments not in their superior and finer degrees, but in the average measure in which they are possessed by a community —a measure which is indispensable for the adaption of the individual to society. Given such a violation of either of these sentiments, and we have what may properly be called *natural crime*." *Id*. at 33–34.

[10] See Part IV: "Outline of Principles Suggested as a Basis for an International Penal Code." *Id*. at 405 *et seq*.

He assumes that a great variety of other offenses will be defined and punished. Indeed, he makes the rather extraordinary assertion that "Beyond question, every disobedience
to law should be attended with a penal sanction. . . ."[11] In
this connection, however, he advances the interesting suggestion that in the statutes such "police offenses" might better be included in a separate code from that dealing with
natural criminality. For Garofalo, however, the chief function of the natural crime concept is to delimit the area of
conduct of major, perhaps exclusive, concern to the scientific criminologist.[12]

Garofalo's concept of natural crime has, as might be expected, produced its critics and its qualified disciples.[13] It
is based fundamentally on the idea that for scientific purposes, the concept of crime cannot be accepted as a legal
category since the factors which produce the legal definitions of crime are contingent and capricious and display no
consistent, unifying principle.[14] The motivation is clear;
yet, it may be doubted that so complete an elimination of
the legal content of the concept has served well the development of criminological theory. Certainly, the efforts to ob-

[11] *Id.* at 34.

[12] This is perhaps stated most clearly in *id.* at 47.

[13] See, *e.g.*, DE QUIROS, *op. cit. supra* note 1, at 28; FERRI, *op. cit.
supra* note 6, at 80; TARDE, PENAL PHILOSOPHY 69 *et seq.* (Howell
transl. 1912). And see HALL, GENERAL PRINCIPLES OF CRIMINAL
LAW 547 *et seq.* (1947); Tappan, *Who Is the Criminal?* 12 AM.
SOC. REV. 96 (1947).

[14] See, *e.g.*, CRIM. at 4. And note the comment of TARDE, *op. cit.
supra* note 13, at 72: "The most striking thing to be here observed
is the sight of an evolutionist making this desperate effort to attach
himself to some fixed point in this unfathomable flood of phenom-
ena and cast anchor exactly in what is the most fluid and evasive
thing in the world, that is to say, feeling."

tain agreement on a definition of crime in purely naturalistic terms have not proved to be conspicuously successful as the controversies that continue to agitate theory demonstrate. The condemnation of conduct through the agencies of government is a relevant social fact of the greatest importance. Any theoretical system which ignores or unduly minimizes considerations of such relevance and importance is likely to produce results which are partial and unsatisfactory. Moreover, this tendency may produce positive dangers in its practical applications. For a consideration of measures that impose stringent disabilities on individuals cannot safely be isolated from the legal and political values. Even within the assumptions of his concept of natural crime, Garofalo cannot escape legitimate criticism. Thus it is probably true that an analysis that attaches the idea of criminality only to violations of the moral "sentiments" of pity and probity is incomplete and insufficiently sophisticated. One doubts, for example, whether the particular horror often associated with certain kinds of sexual offenses can be completely or adequately explained as a manifestation of pity for the victim.[15] Nor do these categories comfortably encompass serious political crime, particularly in a period of intense political conformity when conceptions of morality are identified in significant measure with patriotic sentiments.[16]

[15] *Cf.* "In other words, a failure to punish a criminal is a kind of threat to the repressions which each person places upon his own id." GRIFFITH, AN INTRODUCTION TO APPLIED PSYCHOLOGY 265 (1934). An interesting account of public reaction in early nineteenth-century England to prisoners condemned to the pillory for the crime of homosexuality may be found in ARMITAGE, HISTORY OF THE BOW STREET RUNNERS 175–80 (1933).

[16] Garofalo deals at some length with political crimes and notes that ". . . the act which is normally a political crime may become

Nevertheless, Garofalo's concern with actual problems of legislation and administration, which we have already noted, tends to counterbalance many of the more dubious tendencies of his theory. Furthermore, in emphasizing the relevance of "moral sentiment" to the problem of defining criminal behavior, the concept of "natural crime" has a continuing relevance, even though probably not precisely that which Garofalo intended. Certainly, the modern legislator, like Garofalo, can gain little solace or assistance from the shibboleth that crime is whatever the legislature says it is. For the legislator, particularly at a time when governmental power invades more and more aspects of social life, there are few problems of policy more pressing than identifying and reconciling the social interests to be protected by governmental power, determining which of these interests can sensibly be defended by criminal sanctions, and designing such sanctions in the form most likely to attain the desired ends. No perceptive legislator believes that he is completely at large in this area. There are certain regularities of social and individual behavior which can be ignored only at peril. Garofalo's identification of serious criminality with immorality suggests one of these limiting factors. His distinction between "natural" crimes and "police offenses" points to one of the most serious problems confronting the expanding welfare state, however imperfectly Garofalo may have understood the complexities of policy in the latter category of offenses. Finally, his insistence that there are problems

---

a natural crime when a society suddenly returns to a condition in which the collective existence is threatened." Writing in a happier time he optimistically observes: "But at the present day the state of war is a crisis of short duration. As pacific activity succeeds to predatory activity, the morality of the state of peace succeeds to that of war. . . ." CRIM. at 39.

here which demand systematic investigation of the underlying facts of social and individual behavior produces an
emphasis of a value that has not diminished with the passing of the years.

Characteristics of the Criminal

In Garofalo's theoretical system, the concept of natural
crime serves the primary end of identifying the true criminal against whom measures of social defense must be taken.
Natural crime is behavior that violates certain basic moral
sentiments. The true criminal is he whose altruistic sensibilities are lacking or are in a deficient state of development.
The concepts of crime and the criminal are thus integrally
related. Garofalo, to be sure, makes clear his conviction that
"our knowledge of the criminal is not limited to his acts."[17]
But it is perhaps this joining of the ideas of crime and the
criminal which leads to the frequent emphasis on the act as
a primary index of criminality. In this respect Garofalo's
assumptions often tend to approach those of classical criminology, however much they may diverge in other particulars.[18]

[17] *Id.* at 66.

[18] See, *e.g.*, Beccaria, Crimes and Punishments (1764, English
printing 1872). This parallelism is most clear in Garofalo's discussion of the murderer and violent offender, less clear in his treatment
of the offender against property rights. Thus, on the latter subject,
he writes: " 'What!' some one may exclaim, 'Would you make no
distinction in punishment between the man who has stolen twenty
francs and the man who has stolen but twenty centimes?'
"My answer is that I do not know, for the question is one which
cannot be decided abstractly. The thing important here to determine
is—which one of these two thieves has the greater criminal apti-
tude, and is thus the greater danger to society? It may well be
the former, but it may quite as well be the latter." Crim. at 299.

It is not surprising that in his efforts to delineate the characteristics of the true criminal, Garofalo should turn first to the views of the criminal anthropologists, particularly those of Lombroso. It is clear that Garofalo approached with great interest and considerable sympathy the then current efforts to demonstrate the association of criminality with certain anatomical and physiological characteristics. He finds, for example, that the undue size of the mandibles is "an unmistakable sign of brutality or violence"[19] and that it is "generally admitted that in criminals, the occipital region exhibits a much greater development than the frontal region."[20] Nevertheless, on the whole, his treatment of these matters reveals commendable caution and a healthy detachment. His ultimate conclusion was that the theories describing the criminal as a distinct anthropological type had not yet been proved. "But what criminal anthropology really lacks," he asserts, ". . . is convincing proof that a given character of the skull or skeleton is found more often among criminals than among persons presumably honest."[21] After reporting the frequency of striking degenerative or regressive characteristics in murderers under his observation, he adds: "Still, these characteristics are not always the same: sometimes it is one which is present, sometimes another. The murderer type cannot be described anthropologically."[22] He was aware, also, of the difficulties inherent in validating hypotheses in this area, for he notes the problem of accurately identifying the criminal and non-criminal "pair" for the purposes of trustworthy comparison.[23]

Having found the emphasis of Lombroso's theories inade-

[19] CRIM. at 71.

[20] *Id.* at 67.

[21] *Id.* at 74.

[22] *Id.* at 77.

[23] *Id.* at 75.

quate for his purposes, Garofalo advances his second major concept, the idea of psychic or moral "anomaly." The true criminal lacks a proper development of the altruistic sensibilities. This lack or deficiency is not simply the product of circumstance or environmental conditioning but has an organic basis. For Garofalo, "There is no such thing as the casual offender—if by the use of this term we grant the possibility of a morally well-organized man committing a crime solely by the force of external circumstances."[24] Moreover, the moral anomaly is to be carefully distinguished from insanity or mental disease. The former is not a pathological condition but rather a "psychic variation" appearing much more frequently among members of "certain inferior races" than in modern civilized societies. That the moral anomaly is hereditarily transmissible he finds "established by unimpeachable evidence."[25] But the precise physical basis of the moral anomaly he is unable to describe. At times he refers to it as the product of "some mysterious atavism."[26] At others, as the result of moral degeneracy of more recent origin. Ultimately, he says, "The only safe conclusion which

[24] *Id.* at 95–96. And see: "Hardly anything could be more inaccurate, in my opinion, than the adage: 'Occasion makes the thief.' To be true, the phrase should be: 'Occasion enables the thief to steal.'" *Id.* at 226.

[25] *Id.* at 92. For the modern reader, the evidence for the hereditary transmissibility of criminal propensities adduced by Garofalo often seems particularly inconclusive and the conclusions derived therefrom at times naïve and unsophisticated. Certainly, these conclusions often appear to ignore alternative explanations which in the absence of conclusive evidence are at least equally persuasive. Thus after noting the allegedly higher frequency of criminality among children of elderly parents, he seems to attribute this phenomenon exclusively to the hereditary transmission of psychic traits attributable to old age. *Id.* at 93.

[26] *Id.* at 99–102, 105–11.

we are justified in forming is that criminals have regressive characteristics—characteristics which indicate a degree of advancement lower than that of their neighbors."[27]

It is apparent that these ideas tend to relegate the social and environmental factors of criminality to positions of secondary importance. Clearly, too, such assumptions profoundly affected Garofalo's conclusions about practical measures of crime prevention and repression. He regarded education as chiefly determinative of the kinds of crime committed rather than as an agency for elimination of crime. He was skeptical of economic distress as a cause of crime though, again, he did not deny that economic conditions may affect the form in which crime is manifested. To sound family environment and religious instruction, especially when directed at the child of tender years, he attributed more significance as preventive factors. But even the latter elements were hardly conceived as being of first importance. "Without doubt," Garofalo writes, "external causes such as tradition, prejudices, bad examples, climate, alcoholic liquors, and the like are not without important influence. But in our opinion, there is always present in the instincts of the true criminal, a specific element which is congenital or inherited, or else acquired in early infancy and become inseparable from his psychic organism."[28] Nevertheless, these "external factors," even if of secondary importance, must be taken into account. He did not doubt that the manifestation of even innate criminal propensities can often be repressed by "a favorable concurrence" of external circumstances.[29] The devising of appropriate measures of repression thus becomes the practical problem of central concern.

[27] *Id*. at 109.   [28] *Id*. at 95.   [29] *Id*. at 97.

But in Garofalo's view, the organic deficiency in moral sensibilities, characteristic of true criminality, varies in significant degree from one criminal to another. These variations make necessary a more particular classification of criminal types before intelligent consideration of repressive measures is possible; for differences in the types require differences in the measures to be applied. Garofalo identifies four basic criminal classes which, though distinct, are yet related in that each is characterized by a deficiency in the basic altruistic sentiments of pity and probity. These four classes are those of (1) the murderer, (2) the violent criminal, (3) the thief, and (4) the lascivious criminal.[30]

The murderer is the man in whom altruism is wholly lacking. The sentiments of both pity and probity are absent, and such a criminal will steal or kill as the occasion arises. This extreme form of the moral anomaly is frequently revealed in the very circumstances of the crime committed. The lesser offenders fall into two major groups: violent criminals, characterized by their lack of pity, and thieves, indicated by their lack of probity. The violent criminal may often be guilty of offenses against the person of the type particularly characteristic of a given locality. Such crimes Garofalo terms endemic offenses. Admittedly, these patterns of criminal behavior are strongly influenced by environmental factors. But though imitation plays a significant part in such acts, the offender is an abnormal man, as evidenced by the fact that even where criminality is rampant such offenses are committed by a small minority of the population. The violent criminal may also commit crimes of passion, sometimes under the influence of alcohol. For Garofalo, such crimes, committed in a fit of anger, are indicative of infe-

[30] *Id.* at 111–34.

rior innate moral capacities. "Moreover," he adds, "it has
been my uniform experience as a criminal magistrate that
men who have taken life under the influence of liquor are
nearly always persons who had sustained a previous bad
character or had been formerly convicted of similar offenses."[31]

Garofalo recognizes that the thieves, his second major
subdivision of lesser criminals, may be more the product of
social factors than the criminals in other classes. Certain
environments, in particular, contribute to crimes against
property. "The limits of such an environment need not be
wide," he writes, "two or three evil companions, sometimes
a single intimate friend are sufficient to lead a youth into
this sort of crime."[32] Nevertheless, many manifestations of
such behavior can only be attributed to "a remote atavism"
and, in other cases, to a general deficiency in "moral energy." Finally, there is the rather amorphous category of
lascivious criminals. Many sexual offenders, he recognizes,
must be classified among the violent criminals. The behavior of others is the result of mental disorder. But fitting comfortably in neither category is a group of sexual offenders,
requiring separate classification, whose conduct is characterized less by the absence of the sentiment of pity than by a
low level of moral energy and deficient moral perception.

THEORIES AND MEASURES OF SOCIAL DEFENSE

In a sense, all of Garofalo's major concepts relating to crime
and the criminal may be taken as providing the preliminary
groundwork for his consideration of social defense against
criminality. Almost the entire second half of the *Criminol-*

[31] *Id.* at 177. [32] *Id.* at 127.

ogy is devoted to a study of the theories and measures of crime prevention and repression.

Garofalo's starting-point in considering the problems of intelligent community response to crime is revealing, for he founds his thought on one of those analogies characteristic of the social Darwinism of his day. In nature, through the processes of natural selection, the penalty for lack of adaptation is elimination. The true criminal by the absence or deficiency of the basic altruistic sentiments similarly demonstrates his "unfitness" or lack of adaptation to his social environment. Elimination from the social circle is thus the penalty indicated. "In this way, the social power will effect an artificial selection similar to that which nature effects by the death of individuals inassimilable to the particular conditions of the environment in which they are born or to which they have been removed. Herein the State will be simply following the example of Nature."[33]

Whatever may be said concerning the integrity of the analogy so drawn, it clearly produces assumptions of the greatest importance in Garofalo's thought. In the first place, the emphasis on elimination results in a theory of penalties or treatment which makes incapacitation of the criminal the consideration of central importance. Thus, at the outset, deterrence of potential offenders and reformation of the criminal are relegated to positions of secondary or incidental significance. Second, the analogy relating criminal penalties to "natural selection" is suggestive of the types of penalties which may properly be imposed and, perhaps, serves as a kind of moral justification for criminal punishment by identifying it with the scheme of the natural universe.

It is upon these basic assumptions that Garofalo con-

[33] *Id.* at 219–20.

structs his program of criminal sanctions. Although his proposals are elaborated at considerable length, they can be stated in their essence rather succinctly. The fundamental purpose to be sought is the elimination from society of those who because of moral anomaly are incapable of social adaptation. The surest and most efficient form of elimination is death. And death is the sanction which is clearly indicated when the offender has demonstrated his complete absence of moral sensibilities and is therefore "forever incapable of social life."[34] While there should be no hesitation to apply the death penalty in such cases, the moral sentiments of the community will not permit its imposition on offenders in whom the psychic anomaly appears in a less extreme form. For, as Garofalo observes, "the death penalty has always excited public indignation when inflicted for offenses not seriously violating the moral sense."[35] For these lesser offenders some measure of adaptation is always possible, and the practical problem is to find the environment which will make adaptation probable. Here again, the question is one of degree, and elimination may be relative as well as absolute. There are some—such as certain types of violent criminals, professional thieves, and habitual criminals in general —who are incompatible with any civilized environment. Elimination in these cases must take the form of life imprisonment or transportation overseas. The latter, where available, is much to be preferred on the grounds both of security and humanity. In dealing with young offenders and those whose behavior has been strongly influenced by environmental factors, commitment for indefinite periods in penal agricultural colonies may be indicated. There are also cases where elimination need go no further than the expul-

[34] *Id.* at 224.   [35] *Id.* at 223.

sion of the offender from his particular social situation which may accordingly involve the permanent loss of rights to practice a given profession (where those rights have been abused) and the denial of certain civil and legal privileges. Finally, there are offenders who have committed true crimes but in whom the moral anomaly has revealed itself much less clearly. Here the appropriate sanction is enforced reparation. Damages are to be assessed so that they are sufficient to cover not only the complete indemnification of the injured party but also the expenses incurred by the state as a result of the offender's dereliction. If the offender's means are inadequate, his labor must be devoted to the required reparation.[36]

Even this brief recital of Garofalo's program of repressive measures casts considerable light on his purposes and assumptions. For example, his conviction that legal sanctions ought to be modeled upon a consideration of the psychic characteristics of the particular offender and his dissatisfaction with the conventional penal measures in this respect are clearly shown. As disclosed by his advocacy of the completely indeterminate sentence and particularly the ex-

---

[36] Garofalo's idea of "enforced reparation" is one of his most interesting contributions. Included as an appendix to the English translation is a paper on the subject submitted by him to the International Penitentiary Congress of Brussels in 1900. *Id.* at 419–35. *Cf.* Lex, *Restitution or Compensation and the Criminal Law*, 34 L. MAG. AND REV. 286 (1909); BATES, PRISONS AND BEYOND 292–94 (1938); MICHAEL & WECHSLER, CRIMINAL LAW AND ITS ADMINISTRATION 537–40 (1940). The views of Bentham on "pecuniary satisfaction" also provide an interesting comparison. See BENTHAM, THEORY OF LEGISLATION 282 *et seq.* (Eng. ed. 1871). It should be noted that Bentham receives only one rather disparaging reference in the CRIMINOLOGY (at p. 55), and Garofalo demonstrates no great familiarity with his work.

pansion of capital punishment, stern penalties were for him
an essential ingredient of a rational criminal code. That he
desired as broad a use of the death penalty as it has sometimes been supposed is less clear, however; for he does not
estimate the fraction of the total criminal population consisting of those totally bereft of altruistic sentiments which
make up the class eligible for capital punishment.

But a satisfactory appraisal of Garofalo's thought on these
matters requires a more particular examination of his theories of punishment and his analysis of competing penal philosophies. A comparison of his position with certain of the
postulates of classical criminology may be particularly in-
structive. Garofalo at the outset reveals fundamental theoretical differences with the classical school in his unequivocal
rejection of the idea of moral responsibility as a basis for
criminal liability. Consistently with the positivist position,
he rejects the notion of freedom of the will and accepts a
thorough-going determinism.[37] To Garofalo the idea of
moral responsibility is basically inconsistent with the objective of social defense, for it is the offender least capable of
making and acting upon moral judgments who is most dangerous to social interests. ". . . [W]hen we undertake to as-
certain whether a man is really responsible for what he
does," he writes, "we always end by discovering that he is
not. It is the fallacy which pervades the entire system that
the present ineffectiveness of repression is due. The whole
blame rests upon the two principles of moral responsibility
and penal proportion."[38]

---

[37] *Cf.* the statement of Ferri in his chapter entitled "The Positive
School of Criminology": "Positive psychology has demonstrated
that the pretended free will is a purely subjective illusion." FERRI,
op. cit. supra note 6, at 38.

[38] CRIM. at 337.

Since Garofalo's day the concept of responsibility has proved a persistent source of acrimony and controversy. Without agitating these issues further, it may be relevant, first, to suggest that the explicit rejection of the idea of moral responsibility presented Garofalo with certain theoretical difficulties and, second, to question whether he succeeded in consistently maintaining the determinism he asserted. Given the important role of "moral sentiments" in his conceptions of both crime and the criminal, Garofalo's determinism produced for him the formidable task of separating the idea of morality from that of moral responsibility. He approaches this task by advancing what might be termed an aesthetic theory of moral values. We feel admiration for physical virtues, such as beauty, strength, and grace, and are repelled by the absence of these qualities quite independently of whether the individual possessing any of these traits is free to have other virtues or defects. This is equally true of the moral qualities. "The praise of virtuous and the blame for vicious acts really presents the same case. . . . 'Merit' and 'demerit' have always relation to acts dependent upon moral qualities. The words themselves require no change. All that is needed is a correct understanding of their meaning."[39] An interesting test of Garofalo's position relates to the treatment of the insane criminal. Garofalo emphatically insists that although the insane offender is a criminal and may be quite as dangerous as any other offender, capital punishment must not be imposed upon him. This withholding of the death penalty, which is completely consistent with the classical conception of responsibility, would appear, at least initially, to involve Garofalo in contradiction. But Garofalo denies any inconsistency. A necessary requirement

[39] CRIM. at 304–5.

for the imposition of capital punishment, he says, "is that sympathy for the criminal has ceased to exist."[40] What is the source of this sympathy for the insane man which persists despite the danger of his acts? Garofalo first replies that we recognize in him a potential capacity for social life: "Insanity does not engender a permanent moral character: the perversity in this case is transient and capable of change."[41] But surely, many insane offenders, under the present state of knowledge, display at least as unfavorable a prognosis as those whom he would consign to the death penalty. Garofalo's ultimate refuge seems to lie in the almost metaphysical distinction "between the natural instincts innate in the individual, the instincts which go to make up his real or irreducible character, and [in the case of the insane] the adventitious instincts resulting from physical deterioration."[42]

In turning to his explicit consideration of competing penal philosophies, the modern reader will discover some of Garofalo's most interesting insights. Naturally enough, he rejects the idea of vengeance or moral expiation as a sufficient theoretical basis for penal sanctions. Nevertheless, he finds sound historical basis for the notion that criminal penalties represent in some measure a manifestation of socialized vengeance. Nor is he at all hostile to the sense of outrage and repugnance produced in honest men by the true criminal. For the feeling of outrage provides the social mechanism through which the rational goal of elimination is reached, however imperfectly this may be understood by the public at large.[43]

---

[40] Crim. at 282.   [41] *Id.* at 283.   [42] *Id.* at 284.

[43] "Public sentiment thus coincides with the rational method of social reaction and, perhaps unconsciously, has no other tendency

Garofalo's conception of criminality as something organic and innate in the offender leads, as might be expected, to a considerable skepticism of the possibilities of reformation through education or other modes of treatment. Actually, some of his proposals, which we have already noted, for handling offenders whose crimes reveal a considerable environmental influence are perhaps more in accord with the rehabilitative ideal than he himself suspected. Moreover, his emphasis on the individualization of punishment has probably placed his influence, in the long run, on the side of the correctionalists. Nevertheless, his criticism of the reformative theory is an essential part of his thought, and his observations on this subject even yet supply a useful antidote for the more utopian and irresponsible assertions of some of the correctionalists. At the outset he avoids the error, too often committed, of conceiving that any system of enforced treatment, whatever its motives and purposes, can be stripped of punitive aspects. "The mere deprivation of liberty, however benign the administration of the place of confinement, is undeniably punishment."[44] He notes, furthermore, that the existence of other social goals and values places limits on what may be done in the interest of reformation, assuming that the latter can be accomplished. Nor should the prosaic problems of the public purse or the matter of personnel be ignored. "Where are we to find a sufficient number of these soul-physicians?" he asks. "And what of the expense of such an undertaking?" And would the

_____

than that of bringing about the same effect. It is important however, to notice that this tendency is not the direct result of any process of reasoning by which is demonstrated the social utility of elimination. . . ." *Id.* at 234.

[44] *Id.* at 256.

cure effected by this "moral therapy" survive the offender's return to his old haunts? Fundamentally, however, Garofalo's objections are based on his conviction of the fixity of character types. His hopes for substantial progress were largely confined to reformative programs of the Elmira type directed to the very young offender.[45]

But perhaps most interesting and significant are Garofalo's analysis and criticism of the classical theories of deterrence. Although he ultimately rejects the deterrence of potential offenders as an adequate theoretical basis for criminal penalties, he reveals a more perceptive understanding of the theory than is often displayed by its critics. He recognizes, at the outset, that justification for the deterrent theory need not be based solely on the direct intimidatory effect produced on potential offenders by the threat of penal sanctions. Rather, in more subtle fashion the criminal penalties may regulate behavior by producing and reinforcing general moral attitudes toward certain forms of conduct. Thus the law, by making such behavior unrespectable, subjects the individual to powerful extra-legal sanctions. "No doubt for many persons, the consciousness of the evil involved would destroy any pleasure which the criminal act might afford and is therefore sufficient to cause abstention from crime. But even these persons involuntarily think of the extra legal social reaction attendant upon the offense, namely, by their honest neighbors; and this thought is continually strengthening their resolution to abstain from the acts in question." Without the stimulus of these sanctions, the moral sentiments "would tend to weaken and even, in the course of time, might altogether disappear."[46]

It is apparent, therefore, that in this regard Garofalo's

[45] *Id.* at 266–67.   [46] *Id.* at 241–42.

rejection of the position of classical criminology was by no means complete. Indeed, an important part of his justification for the use of the death penalty in proper cases is the assumed intimidatory result. Nevertheless, deterrence, while an important and desirable effect of criminal penalties, cannot be accepted by Garofalo as the proper criterion of punishment. This conclusion is reached on the interesting ground that the deterrent theory offers no clear standards by which either the kind or amount of punishment can be determined. How is the legislature to measure in advance the quantum of punishment necessary to prevent a given form of conduct in the various social circumstances in which it may appear?[47] How is the danger to social interests of such behavior to be reflected proportionately in the penalties applied? This inherent uncertainty may result either in an excess or a deficiency of punishment. In times of stress and insecurity the effort to deter may result in draconian measures with consequent injury to individual and social interests. On the other hand, the stipulation of the quantum of punishment in advance often requires the release of still-dangerous offenders to the community. For Garofalo, the only rational criterion is that which measures the penalty by reference to the characteristics of the particular offender.

Certainly, Garofalo's analysis of deterrence has point and relevance. The difficulties he suggests are real. Although the

[47] These difficulties did not escape the classical writers. See, *e.g.*, BECCARIA, *op. cit. supra* note 18, at 30: "If mathematical calculation could be applied to the obscure and infinite combinations of human actions, there might be a corresponding scale of punishments, descending from the greatest to the least; but it will be sufficient that the wise legislator mark the principal divisions, without disturbing the order, lest crimes of the *first* degree, be assigned punishments of the *last*." (Italics in the original.)

assumptions of the deterrent theory continue to dominate most criminal legislation, there has been little systematic effort to test and validate these assumptions through empirical study. Few today would assert that considerations of deterrence are in themselves adequate for the construction of a modern system of criminal justice. Nevertheless, it may properly be asked whether in some measure these uncertainties, which Garofalo deplores, are not inherent in any program of action and whether he adequately appreciated the difficulties of his own position. In the first place, it should be noted that for the vast area of penal regulation falling outside the confines of "natural crime," Garofalo fully embraces the deterrent theory with all its infirmities.[48] Second, it seems clear that Garofalo never fully appreciates the problematical nature of identifying and evaluating those criminal characteristics in the individual which make him a threat to the community. As already noted, Garofalo would identify the extreme criminal primarily by a consideration of the criminal act; in this respect he approaches the position of classical criminology. The lesser criminal, however, is to be identified, at least in part, through anthropological and psychological examination. But little effort is made to demonstrate the adequacy of existing scientific knowledge and techniques for these purposes. The reader is confidently assured that "criminology is quite capable of" making these discriminations.[49] At another point, Garofalo refers to "what

[48] "For the stamping out of these non-criminal offenses, it will employ punishments of greater or less severity as necessity dictates, *keeping principally in mind their intimidatory effect*—their influence as an example and warning to would-be wrongdoers." (Italics added.) CRIM. at 217.

[49] *Id.* at 228.

might be called the queen of proofs—an hereditary history of vice, madness or crime," as indicating something of the method he contemplates.[50] It is impossible to escape the conclusion that his assurances are based on incomplete demonstration. One need not deny the relevance of scientific knowledge and methodology to the treatment of the criminal or the prevention of crime to recognize that the real utility of such knowledge is dependent upon a critical appraisal of its limitations. Nor is it necessary to labor the point that a penal system can place basic values in jeopardy by assuming the existence of non-existent or unavailable techniques. That Garofalo was less than sensitive to these dangers can hardly be denied.

Although one of the conscious and explicit purposes of Garofalo's *Criminology* was to challenge certain basic assumptions of classical penal theory, a full consideration of his thought reveals much less than a complete rejection of the classical position. This is indicated by his close identification of the concepts of crime and the criminal with attendant emphasis on the act as an index of criminality, by his qualified recognition of the deterrent effect of penal sanctions, and by his attention to the necessity for some ordering of penalties. These correspondences may suggest that when emphasis is directed to the real and recurring problems of criminal administration, there are wider possibilities for attaining practical reconciliation of diverging theoretical viewpoints than is sometimes assumed.

Nevertheless, Garofalo's differences with the classical writers, such as Beccaria, are frequent and important. Two of general significance should be noted. First, there is in Garofalo's work a recognition of the relevance of the scientific method which rarely receives a comparable emphasis

[50] *Id.* at 388. See also *id.* at 66, 112.

in classical criminology. This is not to deny that Garofalo's thought is pervaded by certain untested, a priori assumptions and that many of his views so based have not survived the passing of the years. Yet his devotion to the ideal of empirical investigation provides a mechanism for the adjustment of hypothesis and theory to new knowledge as it is acquired.

Second, in contrast to the classical writers, there is in Garofalo's thought a persistent tendency toward the exaltation of social interests and a devaluation of individual rights. Both Beccaria and Garofalo, interestingly enough, accept the concept of necessity as the justification for criminal penalties.[51] But necessity means something quite different for each. Beccaria assumes the dominance of individual rights and accepts penal restraints only to the extent required for social coexistence, which, in turn, leads to a fuller realization of individual rights. But Garofalo reveals scant sympathy for any view which accords priority to interests other than those of the group. "Metaphorically speaking," he writes, "the individual represents but a cell of the social body."[52] Nowhere does this tendency appear more clearly than in his discussion of criminal procedures. Recognizing that the procedures he discusses are founded on a very different tradition from our own and that criticism by one foreign to that experience is perilous, one cannot help but be struck by the fact that Garofalo's whole attention is directed to the more efficient apprehension and conviction of offenders. Mistaken or malevolent uses of state power as possibilities which demand safeguards play no part in his analysis. This faith in the benevolence of political authority no doubt

[51] Compare BECCARIA, *op. cit. supra* note 18, at 17–19 with CRIM. at 270–73, 299–308.

[52] CRIM. at 224. See also *id.* at 302, 306–8, 368.

shows that Garofalo was a child of his times.[53] But in less happy days we are not free to make the same easy assumption. Accordingly, the sense of political realities which pervades the thought of Beccaria and his school has a relevance for the present which it obviously lacked for Garofalo.

A full appreciation of Garofalo's contribution requires a more extensive consideration than I can give here of a number of specifically legal topics. His discussion of criminal attempt, for example, remains one of the classic treatments of that difficult subject. His perceptive criticism of the idea of premeditation and his efforts to incorporate a more specific reference to motive in criminal legislation are notable and require attention in any modern effort to restate the penal law.

Admittedly, an appraisal of the continuing significance of Garofalo's *Criminology* must conclude that, despite the value of its insights, many of the assumptions and a great deal of the theoretical apparatus have lost much of their relevance for modern thought. But in addition to its very real contributions, the work retains its power to stimulate; the issues it raises are real and persistent. Perhaps this is enough to ask of any book.

[53] It is worth noting, however, that Garofalo took vigorous exception to the socialism of certain members of the Italian school, particularly Ferri. The latter, for example, wrote: "Sociology will be socialistic or it will not exist." FERRI, *op. cit. supra* note 6, at 17, n. 2. A contemporary account is interesting in this connection: "His [Garofalo's] latest volume, entitled 'Socialist Superstitions,' has excited much wrath and astonishment in socialistic and anthropological camps, and was severely combatted, especially by Ferri, who wrote a pamphlet on purpose to confute the publication. R. Garofolo [*sic*] was born in Naples, in 1852, of an old patrician family, hence perhaps by atavism he is debarred from being a socialist." Zimmern, *Criminal Anthropology in Italy*, 10 GREEN BAG 342, 382, 385 (1898).

REFLECTIONS ON HANGING

CLEON: Let them now therefore be punished as their crime requires. . . . Punish them as they deserve. . . .

DIODOTUS: Now of course communities have enacted the penalty of death for many offences far lighter than this: still hope leads men to venture, and no one ever yet put himself in peril without the inward conviction that he would succeed in his design. . . . Either then some means of terror more terrible than this must be discovered, or it must be owned that this restraint is useless. . . .[1]

THUCYDIDES

In the United States, at intervals of about once each generation, the issue of capital punishment captures fleeting public attention. There are indications that we may at present be approaching another such period. Ordinarily, interest, when aroused, is not very serious and its consequences are less than momentous. The situation in England has been different. For, in a very real sense, the effort to abolish the death penalty in that country has been a continuous one since the days of Romilly and Bentham. *Reflections on*

Published originally as a review of KOESTLER, REFLECTIONS ON HANGING (1957) in 10 STAN. L. REV. 595–605 (1958). Reprinted by permission.

[1] THUCYDIDES 166–67, 169–70 (Modern Library ed. 1951).

Hanging by Arthur Koestler, the well-known novelist and essayist, is part of the polemical literature produced in the latter stages of the abolition movement, a movement that came to climax, or anticlimax, in the passage of the English Homicide Act of 1957.[2] The act, characteristically enough, is a compromise. Capital punishment is not totally abolished, but the death penalty for homicide is limited to five more-or-less intelligible categories of murder.

The contents of Mr. Koestler's book first appeared in serialized form in the English newspaper, *The Observer*. His publisher asserts that these articles made a substantial impression on British public opinion "and materially influenced the course of English law." This may be true. For the author writes with skill and with the passion and intensity of a man who was himself once under sentence of death. It is, however, a curiously uneven work. Its virtues lie neither in the originality of its thought nor in the novelty of its data. Mr. Koestler relies heavily on the materials contained in the *Minutes and Reports of the Select Committee on Capital Punishment*[3] and the *Report of the Royal Commission on Capital Punishment*.[4] It is no more than accurate to say that, for the serious reader, Mr. Koestler's book adds little to the original sources. Perhaps the most "original" portion of the book, a chapter entitled "Free Will and Determinism," is the least successful. The author's excursion into this area is no more, perhaps even less, edifying than most discussions of the same theme.

The literature of capital punishment presents its own particular difficulties and its peculiar frustrations. Almost im-

[2] Homicide Act, 1957, 5 & 6 Eliz. 2, c. 11.

[3] 1930–31. [4] 1949–53.

mediately one detects that the polemics of abolition are pervaded by a curious dualism. There are, first, the *arguments*
against the death penalty. Ordinarily they are of a utilitarian character: capital punishment does not deter crime
and its consequences are detrimental to social welfare. Second, and usually of much greater importance in accounting
for the zeal of the advocacy, is a position founded on certain conceptions of moral value and humanitarian sentiment. The latter, despite its priority, is rarely stated fully
or precisely. And to do so, while presumably not impossible,
is at least difficult.[5] This position, for example, does not
necessarily depend on the theory of the absolute value of
human life or on a Tolstoian doctrine of non-violence.[6]
Sometimes complicating analysis of the abolitionist position
is a further attitude which, while not unrelated to the moral
repugnance induced in many by the death penalty, is nevertheless distinct from it. It is based on assumptions as to the
nature of human behavior that result in a sense of dissatisfaction and unease with the entire concept of criminal responsibility and, indeed, of moral responsibility.[7] All these
factors, in a large measure unanalyzed and unarticulated,
bedevil communication and clear understanding. They appear in Mr. Koestler's discussion, as elsewhere in the liter-

[5] Professor Herbert L. A. Hart has presented a thoughtful discussion of these matters. Hart, *Murder and the Principles of Punishment: England and the United States*, 52 Nw. U.L. Rev. 433 (1957).

[6] See WILLIAMS, THE SANCTITY OF LIFE AND THE CRIMINAL LAW
(1957); see also *Symposium: Morals, Medicine and the Law*,
31 N.Y.U.L. Rev. 1157 (1956).

[7] But that even a position of "hard determinism" does not necessarily result in hostility to the death penalty is abundantly demonstrated by GAROFALO, CRIMINOLOGY 223–25 (Millar transl. 1914).
See also discussion pp. 78–79 *supra*.

ature on capital punishment. In fairness it may be said that he is not unaware of these difficulties and that, if he is not successful in fully resolving them, his failure is not unique.

There are other curious aspects of the capital punishment question worthy of notice. It would be difficult to name any other issue of law reform that presents so many subsidiary areas of inquiry. If, like Mr. Koestler, one is to argue for abolition of the death penalty, one must probe the many pathological spots in the structure of criminal law administration, one must consider the rationale of punishment, one must deal with statistics, with history, ethics, and philosophy. The disturbing thing in all this is the fact that, measured by utilitarian standards, many of the "incidental" issues inherently involved in the abolition debate are considerably more important than the elimination of the death penalty itself. Moreover, the death penalty debate does not provide the best context for discussion of these issues.

Consider one example. A prime and telling argument in the abolitionist's brief relates to the problem of the conviction of the innocent. Defendants are mistakenly convicted, and if they are put to death the mistake is irrevocable.[8] Mr. Koestler, with considerable zest, marshals well-authenticated instances of the hanging of the innocent, not for the purpose of considering ways and means of eliminating erroneous convictions, but to demonstrate the necessity of dispensing with the death penalty. Yet if the factors producing such miscarriages of justice could be confronted and effectively eliminated, the enhancement of the decency and

[8] There probably is no reason to doubt that this problem is more serious in the United States than in England. The leading discussions are BORCHARD, CONVICTING THE INNOCENT (1932) and FRANK & FRANK, NOT GUILTY (1957).

efficiency of the criminal-law processes would represent an achievement overshadowing almost any other conceivable one. Moreover, in the heat of advocacy, Mr. Koestler and others of like mind express a fatalism about the solution of these underlying problems that represents no contribution to their ultimate solution. It is, of course, not possible to solve all problems at once, and there may be nothing irrational in seeking one objective at a time. Nevertheless, the fact that the situations advanced as reasons for elimination of the death penalty are often more important than the death penalty itself provides one explanation for the small success of the movement for the total elimination of capital punishment. It is my impression that in the United States, most persons seriously interested in improving the administration of criminal justice would welcome abolition of the death penalty. That they have not made abolition their prime objective probably reflects their judgment that other problems may be more fundamental.

Let us turn to Mr. Koestler's principal arguments. It is probably safe to say that the crucial proposition in the author's case is the assertion that "the gallows is no more effective than other non-lethal deterrents."[9] Logically, of course, there is no reason why this assertion should constitute the kingpin of an abolitionist position. But realistically, we all recognize that if the abolition movement is to be an effective political force, the no-deterrence point must be persuasively made.

It is a point of very real difficulty. This is true, in the first place, because we are abysmally ignorant about the deterrent effects of legal sanctions in general. We are ignorant, not only bcause an investigation of this problem pre-

[9] KOESTLER 59.

sents formidable difficulties, but because, apart from studies made as contributions to the death-penalty debate, serious empirical investigation has rarely been undertaken. This is in itself a remarkable fact. Rightly or wrongly, most criminal statutes become law on the assumption that their enactment and enforcement will eliminate or minimize the conduct for which sanctions are provided. Yet in a half-century of empirical criminological investigation this important assumption has been largely untested.[10] There are few better illustrations of how a priori beliefs arising from an ideological position[11] may dictate what questions will be investigated. We know, for example, virtually nothing of the actual *mechanics* of deterrence. Must it be assumed that deterrence operates only as a mere threat of force requiring a calculation of pleasures and pains by the potential offender? Or does deterrence result from a more subtle process? Is it possible that criminal penalties may affect behavior by reinforcing popular moral attitudes toward certain forms of conduct, thereby subjecting the individual to powerful extra-legal guidance and control? If so, what is the role of the death penalty in this process? It may be at least worth considering whether this most drastic expression of state power does, in the manner indicated, induce some persons to avoid the whole range of legally condemned acts and not only those directly punishable by death. I hasten to add that I know of nothing which, in the present state of knowledge, would lead one to this conclusion. Indeed, it may be even more likely that calculated and deliberate killing by

[10] One of the rare studies in Andenaes, *General Prevention—Illusion or Reality?* 43 J. Crim. L., C. & P.S. 176 (1952).

[11] See discussion pp. 29–32 *supra*.

the official agencies of a society provides an inducement to violence by individuals.[12] The point is that we do not know.

But if the problem of deterrence has proved to be of comparatively little *theoretical* interest to empirical criminology, the practical necessities of recruiting popular support for the abolition movement have motivated the production of numerous studies designed to test the deterrent consequences of the death penalty. Mr. Koestler canvasses these efforts and rests his argument largely on their results. Although the studies employ several different modes of approach, they arrive at the common finding that, at most, no significant relation can be detected between the presence of the death penalty and the incidence of capital crime. Putting aside studies of such relevant matters as the significance of mental disorder in the commission of capital offenses, these statistical inquiries tend to fall into one of several common types, the most characteristic of which are probably these: (1) studies of capital-crime rates in a particular country or American state before and after abolition of the death penalty;[13] (2) comparative statistics on the incidence of murder in jurisdictions where capital punishment has been retained and those in which it has been abolished;[14] and, less frequently, (3) broader studies of

---

[12] This suggestion is found as early as the mid-eighteenth century. See BECARRIA, ESSAY ON CRIMES AND PUNISHMENT 104–5 (1819 ed.) :
"The punishment of death is pernicious to society, from the example of barbarity it affords. If the passions, or the necessity of war, have taught men to shed the blood of their fellow creatures, the laws, which are intended to moderate the ferocity of mankind, should not increase it by examples of barbarity, the more horrible as this punishment is usually attended with formal pageantry. Is it not absurd, that the laws, which detest and punish homicide, should in order to prevent murder, publicly commit murder themselves?"

[13] KOESTLER 52–53.   [14] *Id.* at 177–78.

general crime rates in abolition and death-penalty jurisdictions.[15] The abolitionist position, it seems to me, would be strengthened if it were frankly recognized that such inquiries rarely approach any minimum standards of decent scientific rigor.[16] Throughout most of his discussion, Mr. Koestler treats these materials with commendable caution and restraint. In the end, however, he cannot resist the conclusion that these demonstrations "prove" the absence of any peculiar deterrent efficacy of the death penalty "as conclusively as the most rigorously sifted evidence can ever prove" any proposition.[17]

If Mr. Koestler had said that many public policy decisions are based on far less knowledge than that which these studies supply as to the probable deterrent effects of the death penalty, few would find it possible to disagree. But the fallibility of such statistical inquiries is obvious, and it is important here to be aware of what we do not know. In the first place, most of these studes require accurate statistics on the numbers of capital offenses actually committed. This presupposes a system of crime reporting that is both accurate and in a form which makes the information accessible. The fact is that, particularly in the United States, these conditions simply do not obtain.[18] But even if such

[15] See, *e.g.*, RUSCHE & KIRCHEIMER, PUNISHMENT AND SOCIAL STRUCTURE (1939).

[16] These matters have been frequently discussed. See, *e.g.*, MICHAEL & ADLER, CRIME, LAW AND SOCIAL SCIENCE 181 (1933); SUTHERLAND, PRINCIPLES OF CRIMINOLOGY 563–72 (4th ed. 1947).

[17] KOESTLER 59.

[18] No doubt, the quality of crime reporting in the United States has substantially improved since WARNER's devastating SURVEY OF CRIMINAL STATISTICS IN THE UNITED STATES (1929) was prepared for the Wickersham Commission. Nevertheless, it can scarcely be denied that American statistics are inferior to those of many other nations and that they are seriously inadequate for scientific purposes.

basic data were at hand, other difficulties would emerge. Suppose, for example, it is shown that in state X murder rates declined in the ten-year period after abolition. Having learned this, what de we *know?* Simply that abolition did not prevent a decline. Whether there is a causal connection between the two occurrences, whether the crime rates would have been the same, higher, or lower had the death penalty been retained, are questions that quite clearly remain unanswered. Comparisons of jurisdictions that have and have not abolished capital punishment are afflicted by similar infirmities.[19] Now, all of this is not to assert that we can derive no useful inferences from such studies. We may say, first, that if additional deterrence results from an application of the death penalty, it is not sufficiently important to reveal itself in these rather crude studies. Again, if the abolitionist fails to show that the death penalty does not deter, no one else has shown that it does. The cautious conclusion of the Royal Commission on Capital Punishment remains probably the best statement of the situation:

... [T]here is no clear evidence of any lasting increase [in the murder rate following abolition] and there are many offenders on whom the deterrent effect is limited and may often be neg-

---

[19] Certainly comparisons of jurisdictions with generally high crime rates, such as certain southern states, with those states that have abolished capital punishment, and which are areas of comparatively low crime rates provide little information about the effects of the death penalty. Comparisons of jurisdictions in which general cultural factors are similar are of greater interest. These latter, even if they do not succeed in measuring the actual consequences of the death penalty, at least strongly suggest that capital punishment as a factor in the incidence of crime is a matter of comparative insignificance. See the conclusions expressed by Professor Sellin, quoted by KOESTLER 178. See also the interesting argument contained in the [CEYLON] COMMISSION OF INQUIRY ON CAPITAL PUNISHMENT REP. (Sess. Paper XIV, Colombo, September, 1959).

ligible. It is therefore important to view the question in a just perspective and not to base a penal policy in relation to murder on exaggerated estimates of the uniquely deterrent force of the death penalty.[20]

There is another aspect of the deterrence argument that deserves attention. There is no reason why an abolitionist must assume, almost as an article of faith, that the death penalty can under no conceivable circumstances enhance the deterrent effects of the criminal law. Rather, the crucial question would seem to be whether one can sensibly anticipate any such consequences, given the circumstances that actually surround the administration of criminal justice. Surely a realization of the deterrent potential of capital punishment, if such actually exists, requires that certain minimum conditions be satisfied. These probably include, at the least, reasonable certainty in the detection and apprehension of offenders, reasonable speed and certainty of conviction, and reasonable speed and certainty in the execution of the death sentence once it is imposed. The incontrovertible fact is that in the United States not one of these conditions is fulfilled today nor is likely to be in the years ahead. No one knows how many capital offenses are actually committed each year in this country. Professor Hart, accepting official estimates, has arrived at a figure of one execution for every one hundred murders and non-negligent manslaughters in the United States for the period 1945–54.[21] Many "murders and non-negligent manslaughters" are, of course, not capital offenses. On the other hand, insofar as the estimates are based upon actual police reporting, the tendency is probably toward understating rather than overstating the

[20] ROYAL COMMISSION ON CAPITAL PUNISHMENT REP. 274 (1953).

[21] Hart, *op. cit. supra* note 5, at 445.

incidence of such crime. But even if the ratio of capital offenses to executions is substantially less than one hundred to one, still the odds that a calculating murderer will escape the death penalty are overwhelmingly in his favor. It would require more faith than most could muster to assume that, when so few of those who commit capital offenses are actually executed, selection of offenders for the death penalty proceeds on anything approaching a rational basis. Quite the contrary appears to be true. Pure caprice must play a large part. But even more disturbing, there is probably a tendency for the selection to be made by reference to unacceptable criteria: the race[22] or poverty [23] of the defendant, the fact that the victim of the killing was a police officer,[24] and the like. But this is not all. Our hesitancy and bad conscience in executing the death sentence, once it has been imposed, must largely nullify any exemplary benefits that could conceivably be gained. One needs only to recall the case of Chessman, who for twelve years successfully delayed the execution of his sentence. Nor is the situation peculiar to California; examples almost as striking are to be found across the land. There is a curious ambivalence in our attitudes toward capital punishment. These delays, this sense of shame in administering the death penalty, must be symptomatic of a widespread distrust of what we are doing. Yet we seem unwilling to act consistently. Indeed, while all of this is going on, we actually add the death penalty to of-

[22] Vold, *Extent and Trend of Capital Crimes in the United States,* 284 Annals 1, 5–6 (1952).

[23] See FRANK & FRANK, *op. cit. supra* note 8, at 86–89.

[24] This appears to be a factor of significance in England as in the United States. See the summing-up of Lord Goddard in the case of Craig and Bentley, set out in BENTLEY, MY SON'S EXECUTION 106–17 (1957).

fenses which were formerly not capital. Congress, itself, has
been a leader in this incredible performance,[25] but Congress
is not alone.[26] Perhaps it is *sufficient* to say that in the
United States capital punishment should be opposed on the
same grounds that induce one to reject any other futile and
foolish course of action.

There are certain other considerations bearing on the
death-penalty debate to which Mr. Koestler devotes no extended attention. Although they are difficult either to demonstrate or dramatize, they may, in fact, be equal in importance to other matters that figure largely in the abolitionist
literature. Some of these considerations may be located by
posing the question: What are the effects of capital punishment on the law and on the institutions of criminal justice? There are reasons to suspect that these consequences
have been serious and unfortunate. There may even be
reason to inquire whether the presence of the death penalty
is today compatible with a system based on the rule of law.
The deleterious effects of capital punishment in the development of the common law of crimes have frequently been
noted,[27] and this at a period when, presumably, popular
attitudes reflected considerably less sensitivity and squeam-
ishness in regard to the death penalty than generally obtains
today. We still suffer from a legacy of legal rules that are
intelligible only as devices to reduce the scope of behavior
subject to the extreme penalty. In the modern period, un-

[25] Thus, Congress has added to the absurdities of American efforts
at control of the narcotics traffic by adding the death penalty to the
already draconian sanctions. 70 STAT. 571 (1956), 21 U.S.C.
§176(b) (Supp. IV, 1957).

[26] See Reifsnyder, *Capital Crimes in the States*, 45 J. CRIM. L.,
C. & P.S. 690 (1955).

[27] See, *e.g.*, HALL, THEFT, LAW AND SOCIETY 118–32 (2d ed.
1952).

mistakable signs of the strain that capital punishment places on a legal order have appeared. Thus, questions of constitutional right have been permitted to turn on whether the petitioner's life is sought by the state. Mr. Justice Harlan, for example, is found saying: "I do not concede that whatever process is 'due' an offender faced with a fine or a prison sentence necessarily satisfies the requirements of the Constitution in a capital case."[28] And for a number of years the constitutional law of right to counsel explicitly distinguished capital cases from those involving other penalties, even life imprisonment.[29] If so much has been done expressly, it is reasonable to believe that much more has been done covertly. And what is done covertly is likely to have consequences that cannot be confined to capital cases.

This is not to say that the abolition of the death penalty will eradicate all motivations on the part of appellate courts to do indirectly what they cannot achieve directly. Thus, so long as courts of review have no power to reduce sentences of imprisonment that appear shocking and unfair, ways and means are likely to be found to reverse criminal convictions on other grounds.[30] But capital punishment adds weighty burdens to the legal process, and the consequences are not all favorable to the social interests that a system of criminal justice is designed to protect.

[28] Reid v. Covert, 354 U.S. 1, 77 (1957) (concurring opinion).

[29] Bute v. Illinois, 333 U.S. 640 (1948); Betts v. Brady, 316 U.S. 455 (1942); Powell v. Alabama, 287 U.S. 45, 84 A.L.R. 527 (1932).

[30] Perhaps an illustration of this is provided by State v. Shobe, 268 S.W. 81 (Mo. 1924). In this case, a conviction for statutory rape accompanied by a sentence of twenty years imprisonment was reversed on grounds of erroneous admission of evidence. The prosecutrix, a professional prostitute, was a married woman and the proof of her age was somewhat vague. She informed against the defendant after a dispute over money.

There is a further point. Mr. Koestler devotes some attention to the effects of the death penalty on those persons constituting the staff of penal institutions where executions occur.[31] The point is a substantial one, especially as it relates to the problem of personnel recruitment for such institutions. Any hopes for a more rational penology must rest ultimately on our ability to create a professional group composed of men of sense and education committed to correctional work as a career. Progress toward this objective has not been impressive. I suspect that one source of difficulty is the presence of the death penalty. It should not be surprising to discover that able men object to participating in the operations of an abattoir.

In short, it seems to me that a reasonable case for the abolition of capital punishment can be made. At best, our handling of the death penalty is futile and not a little ridiculous. At worst, it may be positively pernicious. This is not to say, however, that abolition would be likely to remedy many of the fundamental problems that confront American criminal justice. We would still be possessed of a system that too frequently fails to separate properly the guilty from the innocent; we would still have a system of criminal legislation which is based on no considered or rational principle and a penal system that aggravates rather than reduces the danger of its inmates. Nevertheless, the abolitionist case deserves to be heard. Mr. Koestler's statement of the case is not unexceptionable. But if it directs attention to issues we find too easy to avoid, it will have served well.

[31] KOESTLER 137–38. See ROYAL COMMISSION ON CAPITAL PUNISHMENT REP. 271 (1953). For comments on the effects of execution of the death penalty on other prisoners, see *id*. at 271–72.

CRIMINAL RESPONSIBILITY AND
THE MODEL PENAL CODE

Viewed historically, the issue of criminal responsibility as affected by mental disorder has attracted more attention and stimulated more controversy than any other question in the substantive criminal law. A library of substantial size would be required to house all the literature on the tests of responsibility that has appeared in the English-speaking nations during the past century and a quarter. No one, I am sure, has read all this literature. Indeed, only one with pronounced masochistic tendencies could do so; for much of what has been published on all sides of this controversy is more impressive for its bulk than for its cogency. The enormous expenditure of energy that has been lavished on the tests of responsibility has had its unfortunate aspects. Concentration on this issue and the acrimony it has often produced have tended to obscure the fact that mental disorder creates many problems for the system of criminal justice other than that of determining who shall be relieved of criminal liability and have inhibited efforts to devise solutions to problems requiring practical and thoughtful consideration.

First presented as part of a Symposium on Insanity as a Defense in Criminal Law at Marquette University Law School and printed in 45 MARQ. L. REV. 495–510 (1962). Reprinted by permission.

It may be worth while identifying some of these other problems. There is, first of all, the problem posed by the defendant who is mentally incompetent to stand trial or plead to the criminal charge. The procedures employed in many jurisdictions are wholly inadequate to insure identification of such persons, with the result that in some instances, particularly those involving the impoverished accused, persons incompetent to stand trial are in fact tried, convicted, sentenced, and introduced into state correctional institutions poorly equipped to deal with them. The problems of the incompetent accused are not at an end even when his condition is noted prior to trial, for the "right" not to be tried while incompetent conflicts with another basic interest of the defendant: the right of speedy trial. A defendant who has been confined in a mental institution for months or even years prior to trial may be seriously handicapped in maintaining his defense once criminal proceedings are resumed. Again, there are problems relating to the commitment of persons found not guilty because insane. Assuming that commitments to mental institutions are automatic in such cases (and such seems to be the present legislative tendency), what criteria should govern the ultimate release of such persons? No one familiar with American correctional systems can be unaware that they are rarely staffed or equipped adequately to deal satisfactorily with the problems of mental disorder among inmates of penal institutions. A recent study reminds us that mental disorder may provide tough problems for other aspects of the correctional process, such as the administration of parole.[1] As one gets closer to the problem of criminal

---

[1] Comment, *Criminal Law—Insane Persons—Influence of Mental Illness on the Parole Return Process*, 59 MICH. L. REV. 1101 (1961).

responsibility one observes that the question of who has the burden of proof on the insanity issue is a matter of genuine importance. In some jurisdictions the law (as it should) clearly places the burden on the prosecution once the issue has been raised in a substantial way by the defense. Although the law is clear in such states, many courts at both the trial and appellate levels have refused to apply it seriously, with the result that for all practical purposes the burden of persuasion remains with the defendant. The consequences of this attitude may be particularly serious when the defendant asserting the insanity defense is indigent or of limited means. All of these problems and many more coexist with the problem of articulating a test of criminal responsibility. They must be confronted no matter how the issue of responsibility is submitted to the jury. It would require a good deal of boldness to assert that the practical consequences of the way in which these issues are resolved are in any sense less important than those resulting directly from the differing formulations of the tests of responsibility.

It is, of course, not my purpose in making this recital to suggest that the formulation of the test of responsibility is a trivial or unimportant matter. The contrary is true. At the pragmatic level one of the real reasons for seeking a formulation of a test that commends itself to the various groups concerned with the problem is that the achievement of this goal may go far in releasing attention and energy for the solution of the other problems of mental disorder that insistently require confrontation. It has been suggested by one who observed recent history in the District of Columbia that the way in which the test of responsibility is expressed may subtly influence the way in which other problems are approached even though, analytically, those problems are quite distinct from the issue of criminal responsibility.[2]

But basically the reason for concern with the issue of criminal responsibility as affected by mental disorder is not that this concern may contribute to the solution of other problems. The problem of determining criminal responsibility is a problem in itself and it is important in itself. The function of the test of responsibility is to identify those who, on a calm and sober view, must be regarded as ineligible for the processes of criminal justice with their inherent stigmatic and punitive ingredients and who, therefore, must be conceived of solely as the recipients of care, custody, and therapy. The moral incongruity and the inexpediency of subjecting such persons to the condemnatory procedures of the criminal law are perceptions that have been given some form of expression in the Anglo-American law for the past seven hundred years. It should be noted, also, that the problem of criminal responsibility as affected by mental disorder is not to be approached as a matter *sui generis*, but as part of the broader issues of criminal liability. The insanity defense reflects one of what Professor H. L. A. Hart calls the "excusing conditions" in criminal law[3] and is closely associated with other doctrines, such as mistake, coercion and duress, infancy, and the like. The statement of the insanity defense thus must be of concern to anyone interested in achieving a full, rational, and sensible formulation of the law of criminal liability.

[2] Krash, *The Durham Rule and Judicial Administration of the Insanity Defense in the District of Columbia*, 70 YALE L. J. 905, 907–8 (1961).

[3] Hart, *Legal Responsibility and Excuses*, in DETERMINISM AND FREEDOM IN THE AGE OF MODERN SCIENCE (Proceedings N.Y. Inst. of Phil., 1958).

Not only is the formulation of the tests of responsibility a matter of genuine importance, it is a task of great difficulty. The Reporter of the American Law Institute's Model Penal Code is surely correct when he says: "No problem in the drafting of a penal code presents larger intrinsic difficulty than that of determining when individuals whose conduct would otherwise be criminal ought to be exculpated on the ground that they were suffering from mental disease or defect when they acted as they did."[4] As is well known, the test of responsibility recognized in the overwhelming majority of Anglo-American jurisdictions is the *M'Naghten* rule, supplemented in some American jurisdictions by the so-called irresistible-impulse test. The *M'Naghten* rule, either alone or in conjunction with "irresistible impulse," has been subjected to a barrage of criticism that has persisted for over a century and has emanated, not only from medical and psychiatric sources, but from many members of the legal profession, as well. I must say frankly that it seems to me that much of this criticism misses the point and reflects a serious misconception of the function which a test of responsibility is called upon to perform. I believe we fall in error, however, if because much of what has been said appears irrelevant and unhelpful, we reject out of hand *all* criticisms of the *M'Naghten* rule. It would, after all, be a rather remarkable circumstance if it should turn out to be true that nothing in the case against *M'Naghten* is worth attention or that the statement of all the judges of England in 1843, in what was essentially an advisory opinion, represents a kind of inviolable perfection.

The *M'Naghten* formulation relieves from criminal responsibility those who do not know "the nature and quality"

[4] AMERICAN LAW INSTITUTE, MODEL PENAL CODE 156 (Tent. Draft No. 4, 1955).

of their acts or who do not know that their acts are wrong.[5] No one, I believe, would deny that one who qualifies under this test should be exculpated. It must be clear that the law is incapable of deterring one who, literally, does not know what he is doing or, if he knows, lacks the capacity to evaluate the ethical and moral character of his conduct. The criticisms of *M'Naghten* are directed to other considerations. The basic attack is that *M'Naghten*, applied literally and without distortion, fails to encompass all persons whom justice and good sense would dictate should be relieved of the criminal consequences of their acts. This basic proposition is accompanied by other assertions to which attention must now be given.

It would not be possible and certainly not desirable to recite every count that has been returned in the indictment of *M'Naghten*. But it is important to note a few of them. First, many have urged that the *M'Naghten* rule incorporates an over-intellectualized concept of mental disorder. The key word is "know." Yet, it is said, in many cases of advanced psychosis, cases which everyone would deem appropriate for exculpation, the defendant may have a rudimentary verbal knowledge of right and wrong. What he lacks is understanding of the sort that involves the emotional or affective parts of his personality. In fact, as Dr. Gregory Zilboorg has stated, the separation between the intellectual and affective aspects of personality may be the primary symptom of some types of serious mental afflictions.[6] Some have urged that the word "know" is subject to reinterpretation in the light of modern conceptions of mental disorder

[5] 10 Cl. & F. 200, 8 Eng. Rep. 718 (1843).

[6] Zilboorg, *Misconceptions of Legal Insanity*, 9 AMERICAN J. ORTHOPSYCHIATRY 540, 552–53 (1939).

and that no alteration in the *M'Naghten* formula is required to bring this about. Many careful observers are persuaded, however, that this aspect of the formula is a persistent source of confusion and misunderstanding.

Second, the *M'Naghten* rule is said to be defective in failing to give explicit recognition to volitional disorders; disorders, that is, that deprive the person of control over his behavior. The irresistible-impulse gloss on the *M'Naghten* rule represents an effort to meet this objection. There is a considerable body of opinion, however, which holds that the irresistible-impulse test, at least in its usual formulation, is inadequate. I shall return to this matter very shortly.

The third cluster of objections to the *M'Naghten* rule involves the word "wrong." Some of these criticisms appear extreme and ill-conceived. Thus, one frequently hears it said that psychiatrists are men of science and *qua* psychiatrists know nothing of the concepts of right and wrong. Hence, *M'Naghten* requires them to deal with an inappropriate and uncongenial issue. But surely it must be clear that the expert witness is not called to testify to what *is* right or wrong, but rather to whether the defendant was incapacitated by his mental disorder from making moral and ethical discriminations. The latter is not an ethical question at all. Even if this were less clear, one would be tempted to point out that the moral question in cases in which the insanity defense is likely to be advanced is ordinarily not a very difficult or subtle one. There is a related point, however, of much greater substance. Some psychiatrists, including Dr. Manfred Guttmacher, have candidly asserted that in many cases, cases in which it may fairly be doubted that the defendant was capable of conforming his conduct to the commands of the law, it is practically impossible for the expert to determine whether or not the defendant possessed a rudimentary capacity to distinguish right from wrong.[7] This testimony is impressive and its implications are important for the problem at hand.

Fourth, *M'Naghten* is said to be defective because it requires a *total* incapacity to evaluate the moral character of one's behavior. There is persuasive evidence that such total and absolute incapacity rarely exists even in seriously disturbed persons, including those who are not fit subjects for the peno-correctional process.

Fifth, it is frequently asserted that *M'Naghten,* by focusing on the issue of knowledge of right and wrong, tends to narrow unduly the scope of expert testimony and thereby deprives the jury of testimony useful and relevant to its consideration of the ultimate issue. Professor Jerome Hall, among others, has questioned this assertion;[8] and it is true that we lack a comprehensive factual study of the matter. The fact appears to be that practices of trial courts vary considerably in the scope afforded examination of expert witnesses. On the basis of incomplete knowledge, I find it difficult to conclude that this criticism of *M'Naghten* is wholly lacking in substance.

Finally, a more generalized objection may be mentioned. The deficiencies and ambiguities of the *M'Naghten* rule, it is asserted, induce practices both at the judicial and administrative levels that are not compatible with any reasonable interpretation of the legal rule. The result is the development of a widening disparity between the law in the books and the law in action in this important area, and

[7] *Supra* note 4, at 171–72.

[8] See, HALL, GENERAL PRINCIPLES OF CRIMINAL LAW 519 (2d ed. 1960).

this provides evidence of the need for a sober reconsideration of the written law.

These, then, are some of the points advanced in the critique of *M'Naghten*. It is clear that these points vary considerably in their cogency and persuasiveness. It was the conclusion, however, both of the American Law Institute and of those who participated in the recent revision of the Illinois Criminal Code that the case against *M'Naghten* contains matters of real substance, clearly adequate to justify a thorough-going reconsideration of the traditional tests of responsibility and to provide grounds for a realistic hope that a modern formulation can be devised that would make important contributions to the justice and rationality of the criminal law. The result of this belief and hope is the Model Penal Code test. Response to the new formulation has been encouraging. Although only recently published, it has been enacted by legislation in Vermont and Illinois. A bill proposing the test was adopted by the Oregon legislature but was vetoed by the Governor on grounds that can hardly be regarded as convincing. An advisory commission proposed its adoption in New York, but action was delayed pending a complete revision of the criminal law of that state. A somewhat bowdlerized version of the test was accepted by the federal Court of Appeals for the Third Circuit in the case of *United States v. Currens*.[9] Its influence has been felt on law-revision efforts as far away as Australia. The evidence seems to suggest that the Model Penal Code test will receive wide acceptance in the years to come.

The Model Penal Code provides as follows:

(1) A person is not responsible for criminal conduct if at the time of such conduct as a result of mental disease or defect

[9] 290 F.2d 751 (3d Cir. 1961).

he lacks substantial capacity either to appreciate the criminality of his conduct or to conform his conduct to the requirements of law.

(2) The terms "mental disease or defect" do not include an abnormality manifested only by repeated criminal or otherwise anti-social conduct.[10]

The language of the Model Penal Code reveals several of the assumptions that guided its drafting. First, a test of responsibility should give expression to an intelligible principle. It is the obligation of the law to determine the applicable principle and to express it with all possible clarity and exactitude. There should be full disclosure of the principle to the jury. The jury should not be kept in doubt or be required to infer within what framework of principle its difficult decision must be made.

The formulation succeeds in achieving these objectives with considerable success. Clearly, it is neither just nor expedient to subject to punishment and condemnation persons who, because of their mental disorder, are incapable of responding to the threats and commands of the law. Who are these undeterrables? According to the Model Penal Code, they are those whose mental condition renders them incapable of appreciating the criminality of their conduct or of conforming their behavior to the law's commands. Some, particularly those who support the rule of the *Durham* case, urge that a test of responsibility ought not to include what are characterized as particular symptoms of mental disorder. The reason given is that a reference to symptoms may render the legal test outmoded as new knowledge of human behavior is acquired. With all deference I suggest that such a proposition reflects a fundamental mis-

[10] *Supra* note 4, at 27.

conception of the function the test of responsibility must serve. Unless one is willing to take the view that mental disorder in any degree exculpates, the legal test must be concerned with the particular effects of the disorder on the conduct of the accused. If the principle expressed in the legal formulation is sound, it will not be outmoded by advances in knowledge of human behavior that make it possible to determine with greater certainty and facility whether the mental condition of a given individual places him within or without the scope of criminal liability. If, in other words, it is a sound legal judgment that one who lacks capacity "to conform his conduct to the requirements of law" should be exculpated, this judgment is not rendered invalid by the fact that medical science one day may be able to determine with greater precision that the defendant does or does not possess that capacity.

It will be observed that in its reference to the accused's capacity to conform his conduct to the requirements of the law, the Model Penal Code expressly takes into account impairments of volitional capacity. The test does not use the words "irresistible impulse" and thus avoids the implication that such disorders can be reflected only in sudden or spontaneous acts in contrast to those that are preceded by a period of brooding and reflection. Some proponents of *M'Naghten* deny the necessity of including a reference to volitional disorders in the test of responsibility on the theory that a lack of capacity to control behavior is always accompanied by a deficiency in the intellectual capacity to "know" that the conduct is wrong. It should be observed, however, that much expert opinion casts doubt on the proposition that one lacking capacity to control his behavior by reason of mental disorder will always reveal a deficiency in his intellectual capacity sufficient to produce exculpation under the *M'Naghten* test. But even assuming that incapacities of volition are always accompanied by intellectual disabilities and that these incapacities will manifest themselves in approximately the same degrees of seriousness, there seems to be no reason why a statement of the legal principle should be expressed in terms of the one to the exclusion of the other.

One will also notice in reading the language of the Model Penal Code that it speaks, not of total incapacity to appreciate or conform, but of lack of "substantial capacity." It is not the purpose of this mode of statement to achieve a dramatic expansion of exculpation nor will this be its effect. The purpose rather is to bring the statement of the legal principle into consonance with the underlying facts. As suggested earlier, there are many cases of advanced mental disorder in which rudimentary capacities of cognition and volition exist but which clearly present inappropriate occasions for the application of criminal sanctions. In other cases of advanced mental disorder, no judgment, however expert, can determine whether or not these rudimentary capacities exist. There is real point in a statement of the legal principle that adequately reflects these facts. The truth is that probably most persons acquitted under *M'Naghten* do possess some capacities, however limited, for making moral evaluations of their behavior, despite the requirement of total incapacity. The danger is that if the test does not adequately reflect the reality, caprice and inequities in its administration will result.

It is worth noting also that the Model Penal Code formulation employs the word "appreciate" rather than the word "know." It could hardly be suggested that this verbal refinement is likely to produce any direct consequences in jury behavior. But it may provide a basis for a somewhat broader scope for expert testimony, by suggesting the relevance to the legal inquiry of disabilities in the emotional or affective aspects of defendant's personality. Confusion as to the relevance of these considerations under the traditional *M'Naghten* formula is, it will be recalled, one of the sources of persistent dissatisfaction with the administration of the insanity defense.

One cannot write in any detail about the Model Penal Code test without being required to offer comparisons with another much-discussed formulation, the rule in the *Durham* case. There is much to admire in the objectives of those who support *Durham* and in the concern expressed by the District of Columbia Court of Appeals for the whole range of problems created for the system of justice by mental disorder. But the *Durham* formulation presents real difficulties, and those difficulties must be briefly discussed.

The *Durham* test is "simply that an accused is not criminally responsible if his unlawful act was the product of mental disease or mental defect."[11] These few words have already produced a literature of formidable size. A summary of some of the complaints made about *Durham* may be found in the concurring opinion of Judge Burger in *Blocker v. United States*, recently decided by the Court of Appeals for the District of Columbia Circuit.[12] Probably the feature of the *Durham* test that has attracted more critical attention than any other is the phrase "the product of." True enough, any test of responsibility presents a problem of tracing a causal connection between the mental disorder and the criminal act. But the "cause" element bears an entirely different

[11] Durham v. United States, 214 F.2d 862, 874–75 (D.C. Cir. 1954).

[12] Blocker v. United States, 288 F.2d 853, 857 (D.C. Cir. 1961).

and greater weight in *Durham* than in the Model Penal Code test or the traditional formulations; for in the latter, unlike *Durham*, the jury seeks a causal connection between mental impairment and certain specified effects on the defendant's behavior. If, in determining whether the defendant's act was "the product of" his mental disorder, the jury is invited to speculate on what portion of the conduct was caused by the defendant's "normal self" and what portion of the conduct was caused by the "disease," the formula appears as offensive to contemporary notions of "integration of personality" as the *M'Naghten* formulation it was designed to replace. As the late Judge Brosman of the Court of Military Appeals observed, it is doubtful "that a criminal act can be committed which is *not*, in some sense, a product of whatever mental abnormality may coexist."[13] The point, however, is not that *Durham* results in the wholesale acquittal of criminal defendants who, on one theory or another, ought to be regarded as proper subjects for the peno-correctional process. Here, as elsewhere, an ounce of experience may be worth a pound of speculation; and experience in the District of Columbia does not reveal a startling increase in criminal acquittals. The point is a different one. It is that the product test fails to express an intelligible principle and fails to provide for the jury an adequate framework within which it can exercise its power of decision. This is also the conclusion of Judge Biggs, who must surely be regarded as a sympathetic adherent to the underlying objectives of the *Durham* formulation. In his recent opinion in the *Currens* case, Judge Biggs wrote:

As we have previously pointed out, the psychiatrist, under the *Durham* formula, may give the jury a complete picture of the

[13] United States v. Smith, 5 USCMA 314, 17 CMR 314 (1954).

defendant's mental condition. It is not enough, however, . . . to give the jury a complete picture of the defendant's mental condition. The jury must be further provided with a standard or formula by means of which it can translate that mental condition into an answer to the ultimate question of whether the defendant possessed the necessary guilty mind to commit the crime charged. Our second objective is, therefore, to verbalize the relationship between mental disease and the concept of "guilty mind" in a way that will be both meaningful to a jury charged with the duty of determining the issue of criminal responsibility and consistent with the basic aims, purposes and assumptions of the criminal law.[14]

Judge Biggs added: "The *Durham* formula obviously does not meet these requirements."[15]

Perhaps the point can be further clarified. In 1954 a distinguished committee of the Group for the Advancement of Psychiatry undertook to reformulate the tests of criminal responsibility. The result of these labors was a proposition which, in several particulars, resembles the *Durham* rule. Thus, the G.A.P. proposed that "No person may be convicted of any criminal charge when at the time he committed the act with which he is charged he was suffering with mental illness as defined by the Act, and in consequence thereof, he committed the act."[16] The substantial identity of the phrases "in consequence thereof" and "the product of" is immediately apparent. The interesting thing is that in the published draft of the G.A.P. proposal a footnote was appended to the phrase in question. That note reads, in part, as follows:

[14] *Supra* note 9, at 772–73.   [15] *Id.* at 773.

[16] GROUP FOR THE ADVANCEMENT OF PSYCHIATRY, CRIMINAL RESPONSIBILITY AND PSYCHIATRIC EXPERT TESTIMONY 8 (Committee on Psychiatry and Law Rep. No. 26, 1954).

The psychiatrist can answer the condition—"in consequence of such illness he committed the act,"—not in the sense that mental illness *causes* the crime, but in the sense that mental illness vitiates normal capacity for control.[17]

Notice what occurred. It was apparently felt that some further explanation was required to make the formulation meaningful to the *expert witness*. But what about the jury? The explanation in the footnote was not made part of the formulation. If the additional language is helpful to the understanding of the psychiatrist, if it is part of the essential principle that should govern these cases, what considerations of logic and good sense can justify withholding this statement from the body which must ultimately decide the issue? It is no answer, I believe, to say, as it was said in the *Durham* opinion, that in the final analysis the jury makes a moral judgment about the justice of imposing criminal penalties on the particular defendant. This may well be true. But it is not an adequate reason for leaving the jury at large on the issue or for failing to give it adequate guidance. Surely, there are relevant criteria for the making of moral as well as other decisions. Surely, we are not justified in assuming that the relevant criteria will be immediately apparent to a lay jury called upon to determine the disposition of one suffering from mental disorder who has inflicted serious injury on another. The task we ask the jury to perform is difficult enough without complicating the matter by an inadequate articulation of the principle the jury's action is expected to express.

One other aspect of the Model Penal Code test must be mentioned. No general definition of "mental disease or defect" is attempted, but Part 2 of the paragraph undertakes to say what they are not: "The terms 'mental disease or defect' do not include an abnormality manifested only by repeated criminal or otherwise anti-social conduct." Quite obviously this sentence attempts to deal with the difficult issue posed by the so-called sociopath or psychopathic personality. No doubt, this part of the formulation reflects a number of considerations. First, the widely differing and conflicting criteria employed by practitioners in the diagnosis of the psychopath may be expected to produce peculiarly difficult issues for jury consideration. Thus, as the late Professor Sutherland noted, at one time as many as 98 per cent of the inmates admitted to state prisons in Illinois were diagnosed as psychopathic personalities, while at the same time not more than 5 per cent were so diagnosed in similar institutions in other states.[18] Second, doubts have been expressed about the wisdom of channeling those diagnosed as psychopathic into institutions of medical custody. These doubts relate both to the welfare of the person committed and to the proper functioning of the hospitals to which he would be committed. Third, many have expressed a fundamental skepticism of the integrity of the sociopathic category. Barbara Wootton, an English writer, has recently expressed this view with considerable asperity. Miss Wootton says:

... the psychopath makes nonsense of every attempt to distinguish the sick from the healthy delinquent by the presence or absence of a psychiatric syndrome, or by symptoms of mental disorder which are independent of his objectionable behavior. In his case no such symptoms can be diagnosed because it is just the absence of them which causes him to be classified as psychopathic. He is, in fact, *par excellence,* and without shame or

[18] Sutherland, *The Sexual Psychopath Laws,* 40 J. Crim. L. & Crimin. 543, 550 (1950).

qualification, the model of the circular process by which mental abnormality is inferred from anti-social behavior while anti-social behavior is explained by mental abnormality.[19]

I believe it is safe to predict, however, that much more will be heard on this issue in the years ahead. In the *Currens* case, the court, through Judge Biggs, indicated that in the Third Circuit, psychopathy will be regarded as a mental disease for the purposes of the insanity defense. The same result, of course, has been reached in the District of Columbia, although a recent study asserts that few such persons have actually been acquitted in that jurisdiction on grounds of insanity. It should be noted, also, that the Model Penal Code does not in its terms exclude psychopathy from the definition of mental disease. The label is not outlawed. Presumably a defendant diagnosed as a psychopath may qualify as one suffering from a mental disease so long as the indications advanced to support that conclusion include more than repeated criminal or anti-social behavior.

Let me add a brief word in conclusion. The Model Penal Code formulation creates no revolution. It reflects the traditional insights of the criminal law. Indeed, it reflects those insights more perfectly than the formulations of the insanity defense which are traditionally applied. The Model Penal Code recognizes that the law of criminal responsibility must state a principle that is both intelligible and compatible with the general principles of criminal liability. But the test also reflects a progressive spirit. All is not well with the administration of the law of criminal responsibility, and part of our present difficulties can fairly be attributed to the old formulae. The draftsmen gave careful attention to the specific complaints made of *M'Naghten* and met these objections with, I believe, substantial success.

[19] WOOTTON, SOCIAL SCIENCE AND SOCIAL PATHOLOGY 250 (1959).

CRIMINAL LAW AND THE FUTURE

Despite disappointments and the persistence of a multitude of pressing and unresolved problems, the first half of the twentieth century was a period of genuine achievement for the criminal law and its administration. The principles underlying the juvenile court, parole, and probation gained wide acceptance, and slow progress was made toward their realization in actual administration. Better methods of crime detection and in many localities increasing interest in the effective organization of police systems and police training became apparent. Beginning with the Cleveland Survey, a series of empirical studies of criminal procedure and administration was undertaken in various states throughout the country.[1] The Code of Criminal Procedure was formulated by the American Law Institute[2] and the Federal Rules

Based on an article first printed in 51 Nw. U. L. Rev. 207–17 (May–June, 1956). Reprinted by permission.

[1] CRIMINAL JUSTICE IN CLEVELAND (1922). See also ILLINOIS ASSOCIATION FOR CRIMINAL JUSTICE, ILLINOIS CRIME SURVEY (1929) ; MISSOURI ASSOCIATION FOR CRIMINAL JUSTICE, MISSOURI CRIME SURVEY (1926).

[2] AMERICAN LAW INSTITUTE, CODE OF CRIMINAL PROCEDURE (Official Draft, June 15, 1930).

of Criminal Procedure were adopted.[3] With all their difficulties of scope and method, efforts at scientific study of
crime causation and prevention and the treatment of convicted offenders proceeded at a rate not remotely approached in earlier times. Many items of equal or greater
significance might be added to any such recital.

But the fact cannot be escaped that a list of the characteristic achievements of the period in question reveals an
almost exclusive concern with problems of procedure, administration, and treatment. Apart from an unflagging interest in the issues of criminal responsibility as affected by
mental disorder, there have been, until recently, few efforts
directed at fundamental analysis and reform of the substantive criminal law, and this despite an undeniable and urgent
need for such basic reconsideration. Even in the law schools
where a few did work of the highest quality, not many were
attracted to the area. Indeed, the neglect of criminal-law
studies in the schools is a consistent source of surprise to
foreign observers of American legal education.

There is a paradox here of substantial proportions, and
its further consideration may throw light on where we are
and where we may be tending. It seems hardly possible to
deny the importance of the body of law that authorizes imposition of the most rigorous sanctions at the command of
the state. Nor can it be seriously questioned that careless
and inexpert articulation of penal legislation presents an
often serious threat of injustice to persons and injury to
vital social interests. If the comparative lack of attention
to these problems in the schools be explained by the
assertion that few graduates practice criminal law, it may be

[3] CRIM. PROC. FOR THE UNITED STATES DISTRICT COURTS RULES.
(Effective March 21, 1946, as amended.)

answered that in all likelihood many more lawyers are concerned with the criminal law as practitioners, prosecutors, judges, legislators, governmental administrators, and members of the military than are concerned with some of the more esoteric specialties that have become staples of the law school curriculum in the last generation. If it be thought that the problems are trivial, unduly technical, or lacking in intellectual challenge, one needs only to consider the range of issues presented by legislative reformulation of any considerable area of the criminal-law doctrine to discover that the belief is groundless. Even if one's interests lie primarily in the problems of treatment of offenders and related matters, it should be recognized that the existence of the criminal presupposes a crime and that the problems of treatment are derivative in the sense that they depend upon the determination by the law-giving agencies that certain sorts of behavior are crimes.

Some further explanation for the lack of systematic attention to the substantive criminal law is, therefore, required. The answer, it seems to me, may lie in certain tendencies which dominated social thought in the first half of the twentieth century, although their origins are much older. One of the strongest of these is the positivist bias against authoritative rules in any form and which, in its more extreme varieties, challenges the reality of such rules. The expression of this attitude in legal thought generally has produced a conception of law as a process rather than as a set of rules or authoritative norms. Since the criminal law deals in part with behavior which is also within the immediate purview of other disciplines, attitudes toward the criminal law may have been more directly and profoundly affected by the dominant intellectual tendencies than those relating to other branches of the law. Much in the intellectual currents of our time has been thought to challenge the validity of the basic postulate of the criminal law: the concept of criminal responsibility. At the least, many of the modern tendencies have encouraged even the criminal-law specialist to escape from the problems of substantive doctrine and definition to a refuge in things that "really matter," which is to say, problems of procedure, enforcement, and treatment.

In recent years there is evidence of some change in the situation. In part, this may reflect a shift of emphasis in the general trends of current thought. But there have probably been other factors more directly applicable to the criminal law. It is not too much to say that a great part of the criminological labors of the last half-century proceeded with little consideration of the political and ethical values which are inevitably involved. Perhaps it would be more accurate and just to say that many engaging in these labors simply assumed the existence of a store of such values without undertaking any responsibility to nourish or replenish them. One may search much of the writing in vain for any recognition that the broad and uncontrolled authority advocated over persons is capable of sinister use by political agencies for illegitimate purposes. Mistaken or malevolent uses of state power have rarely been considered as possibilities demanding measures or concern. Unfortunately, the history of recent years has demonstrated all too clearly that the criminal law and its sanctions are capable of use as instruments for the destruction of basic political values and, in the world as a whole, that malevolent use of state power has become rather the rule than the exception. Accordingly, the realization has grown steadily that the values of legality and equality at the hands of the state are of the essence of a free community and that the substantive criminal law has a major contribution to make in their preservation. It has also appeared to some that the problems of reconciling these political values with the advantages of individualized therapeutic treatment of those brought within the scope of state sanctions presents an intellectual challenge of major proportions.

However this may be, it seems likely that the next fifty years will reveal a much more active concern with the substantive criminal law than in the past. Indeed, this activity has already revealed itself in comprehensive revisions of criminal legislation enacted in three American states[4] and, most particularly, in the outstanding advances in thought and articulation achieved by the American Law Institute's Model Penal Code.[5] Confidence in this forecast is strengthened by observing the wholly unsatisfactory state of criminal legislation in this country. The fact that the deficiencies of criminal legislation have reached the point of providing a serious impediment to accomplishing the immediate purposes of the law provides the best guaranty of its revision in the next half-century.

II

The lack of systematic interest in the law of crimes, which characterized the first half of the present century, did not inhibit at all the enactment of penal laws. Indeed, criminal legislation burgeoned as never before.[6] This mass of new

[4] LOUISIANA CRIM. CODE, 1942; WISCONSIN CRIM. CODE ch. 696 (1955); ILLINOIS CRIM. CODE OF 1961 (ILL. REV. STAT. ch. 38 [1961]).

[5] AMERICAN LAW INSTITUTE, MODEL PENAL CODE (1964).

[6] See discussion pp. 3–4 *supra*.

penal statutes has produced an array of problems, some of them serious and difficult. The resolution of these difficulties constitutes part of the unfinished business of the next half-century.

Beginning principally with World War I, almost all American legislatures enacted a variety of laws that may loosely be described as defining "political crimes": offenses that affect, or are believed to affect, the security of the state. Some of the most momentous constitutional adjudications in the modern era have involved interpretation and application of these laws.[7] Since the legislative objective in the enactment of such statutes is to frustrate subversive activity before it constitutes an unmanageable threat to the political institutions, these laws characteristically seek, by use of the conspiracy concept or other devices, to reach conduct that is not immediately injurious but which is deemed to be *potentially* dangerous. It is, no doubt, inevitable that such efforts should be made; but the perils involved should be evident. As the late Professor Ernst Freund observed many years ago, ". . . in the absence of scientific certainty it must be borne in mind that the farther back from the point of imminent danger the law draws the safety line of police regulation, so much the greater is the possibility that legislative interference is unwarranted."[8] Obviously, what the future of this trend will be depends on what the state of the world is to be. One may say with some confidence that, if in the next half-century there is atomic warfare or even the continued nervous apprehension of foreign political and

---

[7] See, *e.g.*, Gitlow v. New York, 268 U.S. 652 (1925); De Jonge v. Oregon, 299 U.S. 353 (1937); Dennis v. United States, 341 U.S. 494 (1951).

[8] FREUND, STANDARDS OF AMERICAN LEGISLATION 83 (1917).

military aggression, the trend with all its perils will persist and, indeed, be intensified.

A second and even more characteristic type of modern criminal legislation is that defining the so-called regulatory offenses: crimes created by legislatures in overwhelming numbers to effect certain objectives of economic regulation or public welfare. Even more impressive than its mass are the problems such legislation produces. The demand for regulatory statutes first reached flood stage in the last half of the nineteenth century, when administrative law was in its primitive phases of development and sophistication. The resort to criminal penalties may often have represented the only apparent means of accomplishing the regulatory purposes. This necessity has abated with the passage of the years and the development of alternative regulatory techniques. Yet as one surveys much modern legislation, one cannot fail to be struck by the lack of ingenuity displayed in devising sanctions. Only too often, the draftsmanship of such statutes is defective, giving rise to wholly avoidable problems of interpretation and application. Often penal provisions have been added to regulatory statutes almost as afterthoughts. Few show evidence that any substantial consideration was given to the need for criminal sanctions in the particular situation or to the possibility that alternative sanctions—equitable remedies, damage actions, license revocation, and the like—might achieve the regulatory objectives more effectively or with less harshness to the affected individuals. This legislative insouciance is illustrated by a story involving one of the most intricate regulatory statutes enacted by Congress in the New Deal period. When the draftsman was asked what considerations underlay the inclusion of rather severe criminal penalties in the law, he is said to have replied: "I don't recall; I can only say they got into the draft late one Saturday afternoon."[9]

The regulatory statutes are important for another reason. Typically this legislation seeks to punish behavior which is not by any means condemned unanimously by the community. For this and other reasons enforcement of this legislation is often extraordinarily difficult. To overcome these difficulties, substantial penalties are often authorized to be imposed on individuals who have not been shown to possess any wrongful or criminal purpose and, in some cases, on defendants who have done all that could be done to comply with the law's commands. This propensity of legislatures to eliminate the requirement of *mens rea* or criminal purpose in the definition of criminal behavior raises substantial issues for legal theory. One may doubt the justice of subjecting to the stigmatic consequences of criminal conviction individuals whose conduct may in no sense be regarded as blameworthy. It may also be doubted whether, in the long run, a definition of the criminal that encompasses persons whose standards of conduct in no way diverge from those approved by the community at large advances the general preventive purposes of the criminal law. There is, of course, every prospect that this area of legislative regulation will continue to enlarge. Inevitably, criminal sanctions will play a part in such regulatory efforts. Recent indications suggest, however, that the next half-century may produce a greater awareness of the perplexities and dilemmas associated with such legislative intervention. The extremities of the present situation may, again, provide the best hope for amelioration.

[9] These matters are canvassed more fully in Allen, *Book Review*, 66 YALE L.J. 1121 (1957).

In considering the future developments of the criminal law, however, one may expect not only expansion, but contraction. Withdrawal of criminal sanctions, in whole or in part, from certain areas may be anticipated with some confidence. Problems of habitual drunkenness, already discussed, may represent one such area.[10] Current efforts at public control of alcoholism employing the traditional devices of fine and imprisonment are distinguished chiefly by their futility. The present situation with all its waste, expense, and frustraton has been tolerated chiefly because of the absence of available alternatives. There is already widespread recognition that the problem is primarily one of medical care and welfare services. Efforts presently being made to devise effective care and treatment in these cases give some promise of more rational and constructive social response in the years ahead. American efforts at control of narcotic addiction through the agencies of the criminal law have given rise to problems which are infinitely more complex and intractable. The absence of reliable statistical data makes impossible any sound estimate of the effects of rigorous criminal sanctions on the incidence of narcotic addiction in the United States. There can be little doubt, however, that such measures have often had the effect of increasing other forms of crime, particularly crimes against property, by addicts seeking money to pay for drugs rendered scarce and expensive by the enforcement of narcotic laws. It is also true that the difficulties and frustrations of such enforcement have sometimes tempted the police into illegal practices and that, in general, our approach to the phenomenon of addiction has been characterized neither by intelligence nor humanity. Only since the 1950's have these

[10] See discussion pp. 7–8, 12–13 *supra*.

facts begun to penetrate the public consciousness. There is reason to expect that demands for fundamental alterations in approach will become widespread. But no consensus has developed as to the new direction our policy should take, and there is no assurance that many of the proposals for reform will not threaten difficulties almost as formidable as those associated with present practices. These problems must be confronted in the next half-century, and few areas are likely to present so demanding a test of our capacity to devise rational policies.

III

The intelligent utilization of a growing fund of scientific insight and technique in the processes of correction and criminal-law administration will very likely become the object of increasing attention in the years ahead. These are, of course, not new questions; but we have only begun the task of understanding and defining the role of scientific technique in the administration of criminal justice. In some degree, fruitful co-ordination of the efforts of lawyers and representatives of other disciplines has been impeded by the century-old controversies surrounding the legal tests of criminal responsibility in cases of mental disorder. One of the most unfortunate aspects of the polemics surrounding the *M'Naghten* rules has been the diversion of attention from other problems of law and medicine hardly less important than the formulation of rules of responsibility for criminal trials.[11] The decision of *Durham v. United States*[12] and the appearance of the Model Penal Code have clarified

[11] See discussion pp. 105–8 *supra*.

[12] 214 F.2d 862 (D.C. Cir. 1954).

the issues involved in formulating the legal tests of responsibility and may have improved prospects for a reasonable accommodation of views. It is certain that the *M'Naghten* rules have been viewed by many as a symbol of the law's obduracy; and intelligent modification of the traditional law may well release new energies for constructive solutions of problems which insistently demand attention.

There have been other causes for the slowness of advance in this area. Perhaps the basic reason is that progress toward a fund of reliable knowledge continues to be slow and painful. New knowledge is the product of systematic investigation, and few would deny that our society has failed to make adequate provision for such inquiry. For all our ignorance we do less well than we know how to do. Proper administration of justice is obstructed by public apathy and the familiar problems of insufficient financial support. Certainly the size and arrangements of our existing institutional structures (many of which, unfortunately, are destined to be kept in use for the next half-century) provide a major obstacle to even the most rudimentary efforts toward rehabilitation. Even so, it can be expected that the next half-century will see much movement in these areas. We may anticipate increased resort to clinical facilities to assist performance of the sentencing function, to psychiatric and other services for diagnosis, classification, and treatment within the penal system, to the diversification of the types of penal institutions, and to experimentation with half-way houses and other programs of supervised release.

The tendency toward individualized treatment of persons within the custody and control of the state, however, creates its own problems and perils. These have already emerged clearly enough to justify the belief that here we are likely to be confronted with some of the toughest issues in the years ahead. Programs of individualized treatment inevitably involve the exercise of wide discretionary powers on the part of administrative personnel who possess, or ought to possess, special skills and proficiency. This, of course, is a situation not peculiar to penology but is a salient characteristic of the range of modern governmental activity. There are surely good reasons for the law's insisting that the discretion exercised in the administration of penal sanctions be at least as responsible as that exercised in the performance of other governmental functions. The fact is, however, that today it is hardly possible to discern, even in rudimentary form, what might be called a body of criminal administrative law. Too often this has meant that in this area we have had administration without law. It is not difficult to multiply examples. Is there any reason why a prisoner returned to a penal institution for violation of parole should not at that time have, as a matter of right rather than grace, a full hearing on the issue of whether the parole terms were, in fact, violated? And, for that matter, should not legislative standards relating to parole conditions be made sufficiently specific to avoid at least some of the technical absurdities of which parole boards have occasionally been guilty in the past? Perhaps more serious are the problems relating to the release of persons in custody under statutes authorizing what is euphemistically called indeterminate "civil" commitment: sexual psychopath laws, defective delinquent statutes, laws requiring automatic commitment of those successfully pleading insanity at the criminal trial, and others. The problems presented are created in a large part by the law itself. Meaningful standards relating to the release of committed persons to the community are often lacking. Pro-

cedures through which a denial of release can be challenged
are, in reality, often largely ineffectual. Without meaningful
standards, administrative personnel are compelled to devise
ad hoc criteria of their own. In too many cases the actual
standards being applied would not, if they were articulated
and subjected to scrutiny, pass public inspection.

These issues are easier to state than to resolve. Much
remains to be done in the way of setting up effective procedural devices within the penal system through which a
variety of decisions relating to methods of treatment, transfer, and release may be subjected to real supervision and,
where necessary, to challenge. In regard to certain of these
decisions, review in the courts should be provided. A desire
that administrative discretion should be subject to effective
supervision indicates no disposition to minimize the significance of expert judgment in the adminstration of the criminal law or a desire to stifle or obstruct its proper exercise.
It indicates, rather, that such judgment is attaining a role
of great importance in penological administration and that
this role promises to be even more significant in the future.
This suggests that the vital interests of the individual and
the state thereby affected require considered and articulate
statements of legislative policy in the field and measures to
insure the advance of that policy through the responsible
exercise of administrative discretion. One may suspect that
there are problems in this area sufficient to occupy the next
half-century and more.

IV

In the area of criminal procedure, no development in the
recent past is of greater significance than the increasing
exercise of judicial supervision over the state systems of

criminal justice by the Supreme Court of the United States. The expanding definition of due process of law under the Fourteenth Amendment has imposed on the states a new catalogue of restraints, some of which were scarcely contemplated as recently as a generation ago. These developments, as might be expected, have proved controversial. It is not difficult to take exception to certain of the Court's decisions or to complain that the emerging constitutional doctrine has not always represented a model of clarity or consistency. Yet it is demonstrable, it seems to me, that during the last generation the Court has made contributions of the greatest value to American criminal procedure and administration. One of the most significant of these has often been overlooked. In the exercise of its supervisory functions the Court has frequently brought to public attention deficiencies in state procedural law and practice and has thereby opened the way to intelligent local legislative response. This is of particular importance because, basically, the problems in this area are legislative in character. It is becoming increasingly evident that, important as the Court's role has been and—one may hope—will continue to be, its function is necessarily a limited one. What can be achieved through imposition by the Court of constitutionally based exclusionary rules of evidence is only a small part of the total solution. If we are to make further significant progress toward efficiency and decency, we shall have to achieve it principally through legislative initiative. And we shall have to recognize that the problems are, in the larger part, not those of the limits of constitutional power but of policy and common sense.

There are, however, a number of issues with constitutional overtones which are likely to engage attention in the next fifty years. Despite the continued concern of the Court with the matter, the problem of the third-degree and the limits of police interrogatory practices persists, and a significant advance toward its ultimate solution has yet to be achieved. Pre-trial comment on pending criminal cases through the media of mass communications represents one of the most ominous threats to efficiency in law enforcement and to the fair trial of the accused. The impact of radio and television has significantly expanded the proportions of the danger. The development of electronics has produced, and will continue to produce, issues of another sort. Already we are approaching the literal confirmation of Mr. Justice Brandeis' portentous forecast uttered a generation ago: "Ways may some day be developed by which the Government, without removing papers from secret drawers, can reproduce them in court, and by which it will be enabled to expose to a jury the most intimate occurrences of the home."[13] Sooner or later, and very possibly in the next fifty years, we may be forced to appraise squarely the value of individual privacy and determine what sacrifices we are prepared to make to preserve it. We may also be confronted with issues concerning the use of narcoanalysis, hypnosis, and lie detector devices. So far, we have been able to avoid the fundamental inquiry inherent in the use of evidence obtained by such means. It has been possible to exclude such evidence from judicial proceedings because of legitimate doubts about its reliability. But this escape will not always be available, and it is entirely likely that, by virtue of perfection of the processes, it will be denied before the next fifty years have elapsed. When that time comes, we shall be required to an-

[13] Olmstead v. United States, 277 U.S. 438, 474 (1928) (dissenting opinion).

swer the sober question whether there are individual values of such great importance that extraction and use of this type of evidence by the prosecution must, despite its scientific reliability, be denied. We may anticipate that these and other questions will be raised in the next half-century. There is no way to know how they will be answered. No doubt, the answers will depend largely on the state of the world. But it is also possible that how these questions are answered may, in some degree, affect the state of the world in the years ahead.

Not all the problems of criminal procedure produce such dramatic issues. But these other problems, in their totality, may be hardly less important. Thus, current procedure and practices in the small-crimes courts have often proved incapable of identifying dangerous and disturbed offenders. At the same time, they frequently create the peril of conviction of the innocent. Such problems rarely come to the Supreme Court or other appellate courts for scrutiny. Consequently, they will be solved, if at all, through local initiative.

Efforts of the last half-century to reform criminal procedure and administration have produced many solid achievements. Yet in looking back on the enthusiasm of the late twenties and thirties one cannot escape the sense of unrealized expectations. This experience may have lessons to teach us for the future. Much of the energy expended in earlier movements for reform was directed to measures which, while often perfectly unexceptionable in themselves, would, even if adopted, have made only slight contributions to the cure of the basic pathologies. It is important to recognize that the administration of criminal law is largely a function of local government. If local government performs its other functions inefficiently and corruptly, there is surely little reason to believe that the administration of law enforcement and the trial of criminal cases will escape the same taint. Great improvements have occurred since Lord Bryce observed: "There is no denying that the government of cities is the one conspicuous failure of the United States."[14] Nevertheless, in varying degrees the patterns of political and economic exploitation which became associated with municipal government during the period of the fantastic growth of American cities in the last century still persist. Obviously, there are many problems peculiar to the local administration of criminal justice which insistently demand attention. Yet our past experience suggests that future efforts at reform of criminal-law administration are likely to prove less than successful if these efforts are separated from the general issues of local government.

In looking ahead to the next fifty years we are less likely to assume the inevitability of progress than our fathers did a half-century ago. Certainly, one concerned with the development of the criminal law finds little to tempt him toward an uncritical optimism. But if the perils and difficulties of the next fifty years seem formidable, the opportunities are even more impressive. Nevertheless, the perils are real. Perhaps the best guidance available to us in facing the problems of the years ahead is that offered the maid in Spenser's *Faerie Queen*. Written on the iron door were the words: *"Be bold, be bold* and everywhere *Be bold."* But on another door appeared the caveat: *"Be not too bold."*[15]

[14] Bryce, The American Commonwealth 444 (Ab. ed. 1896).
[15] Book III, Canto 11, Stanza 54.